DARWINISM, DOGMA, AND CULTURAL EVOLUTION

OTHER BOOKS
BY C. R. HALLPIKE

Ship of Fools:
An anthology of learned nonsense about primitive society

Do We Need God to be Good?
An anthropologist considers the evidence

Ethical Thought in Increasingly Complex Societies:
Social structure and moral development

On Primitive Society, and other forbidden topics

How We Got Here: From bows and arrows to the space age

The Konso of Ethiopia:
A study of the values of an East Cushitic Society

The Evolution of Moral Understanding

The Principles of Social Evolution

The Foundations of Primitive Thought

C R HALLPIKE

DARWINISM, DOGMA, AND CULTURAL EVOLUTION

CASTALIA HOUSE

Darwinism, Dogma, and Cultural Evolution

C. R. Hallpike

Published by Castalia House
Tampere, Finland
www.castaliahouse.com

Editor: Vox Day
Cover Design: Castalia House
"March of Progress" Illustration: Tamburn Bindery

ISBN: 978-952-7065-64-8

Contents

Preface

Every subject probably has its dogmas, beliefs held with certainty not because they are exhaustively researched or self-evident, but because "authority" (or often, more accurately, "group-think") has placed them beyond question. Anthropology has had plenty, for example: that every custom and institution exists because it has some essential function, that there is no such thing as human nature, that all moral standards are relative, that psychology can tell us nothing about culture, and that there is no such thing as cultural evolution (or even primitive society). My fieldwork in Ethiopia and Papua New Guinea helped convince me that they were all nonsense, and that explaining cultural evolution in particular was an intellectual challenge of the first importance.

In the course of this evolutionary research I inevitably encountered Darwinian theory in the form of the sociobiologists and evolutionary psychologists and memeticists, all convinced that natural selection provides the ultimate and unchallengeable explanation of cultural evolution. It soon became clear however that their dogmatic certainty that they were right was only equalled by their ignorance of anthropology, so I have written a short account of why natural selection is a useless theory of cultural evolution, and have tried to give a general but concise explanation of how this evolution actually occurs without having to include all the detailed supporting evidence which can be found in my other books[1].

I have referred to "cultural evolution" but the terms "culture" and "society" need clarification. "Society" refers in particular to social institutions and how people are organised, and "culture" to what they think and believe, and "material culture" to their technology. But social institutions, like "monarchy", or "clan" are ideas too, and so also part of culture, just as material culture is based on social organisation. Culture and society, then, are distinct in theory but in practice must always be found together. The "cultural evolution" of the title therefore includes social institutions, and I often refer to social evolution where I primarily have institutions in mind.

Notes

1. *The Foundations of Primitive Thought*, 1979; *The Principles of Social Evolution*, 1986; *The Evolution of Moral Understanding*, 2004; *How We Got Here: From bows and arrows to the space age*, 2008; *The Konso of Ethiopia*, 2008:219–61; "How social evolution works", 2011a; "Memetics: a Darwinian pseudo-science", 2011b; "The weakness of adaptive explanations", 2011c; "Some anthropological objections to evolutionary psychology", 2011d; *Ethical Thought in Increasingly Complex Societies: social structure and moral development*, 2016.

Chapter I
The limits of Darwinism

Human beings are unique and have become increasingly unlike anything else in the animal kingdom, so it is reasonable to wonder how this extraordinary divergence occurred. Life on earth apparently began some 3.5 billion years ago, but modern humans, *Homo sapiens sapiens*, only appeared about 200,000 years ago, and until about 10,000 years ago the whole human race lived in small bands of hunter-gatherers. By this time the emergence of language had provided an entirely novel basis for human culture, and by "culture" I don't mean simply learning new behaviour and passing it down the generations, which many animal groups can do. I mean the ability to use language to transmit *ideas*—knowledge, values, customs, and beliefs—to other people, by allowing the sharing of ideas and therefore the development of social *institutions*, which are unique to Man. One cannot *see* the Prime Minister, for example, but only a specific person, and someone who does not know what being a Prime Minister *means* has to be told what the role involves and how it fits into the rest of the British Constitution.

The adoption of agriculture led to the emergence of tribal societies of farmers and herdsmen and then in a few thousand years to early agrarian states. By the beginning of the Common Era, in a number of independent and unrelated parts of the world, literate civilisations with very large populations had evolved with a fairly standard set of institutions: sacred hereditary kings; a nobility; professional armies; a class hierarchy; urban civilisation and a market economy with highly developed crafts; writing; bureaucracy; priests or their equivalents; monumental architecture; and a particular interest in calendrical science and astronomy, so that the Chinese, Indians, Persians, Egyptians, Europeans, and Central Americans and the Inca would have found many fundamental similarities in each other's societies. Social change continued to accelerate, and modern science, technology, and industrial society have appeared even more rapidly over the last four centuries. All this suggests that certain basic developmental processes have been at work in human society, but their extreme rapidity, by comparison with the extreme slowness of biological evolution, also confirms that social processes are very different from those of biology. Many evolutionary biologists and their supporters nevertheless insist that the Darwinian theory of natural selection can account for this evolution of human society and culture just as well as it can for the evolution of animals and plants.

1. Universal Darwinism

Darwinists maintain that random variation plus selection is enough to explain the emergence of order everywhere in nature. Random genetic variation or "mutation" produces changes in a plant or animal which affect its survival and reproductive success. If such a change improves reproductive success the change is "selected" and inherited by the next generation, and this cumulative variation and selection over many generations is responsible for the variety of animal and plant species we find today. But Darwin's extremely simple notion of variation and selection has been extended to "a scheme for creating Design out of Chaos without the aid of Mind" (Dennett 1995:50), and that includes human minds and consciousness as well as the Divine Mind. Dennett has described this theory as an "algorithm", a "universal acid", which "eats through just about every traditional concept, and leaves in its wake a revolutionised world-view…" (ibid., 63).

"Universal Darwinism" therefore covers not only biology, psychology, and consciousness but the evolution of human society and culture, and even of the universe as well: so Dennett argues that the physical laws of our universe could also have evolved by natural selection acting on an infinity of different laws of physics over sufficient time (ibid., 177–80). D. B. Kelley (2013) claims that universal selection is the origin of everything and has been operating since the Big Bang "to preserve favoured systems in contention for existence". In Dennett's opinion:

If I were to give an award for the single best idea anyone ever had, I'd give it to Darwin, ahead of Newton, Einstein and everyone else. In a single stroke, the idea of evolution by natural selection unifies the realm of life, meaning, and purpose with the realm of space and time, cause and effect, mechanism and physical law (1995:21).

S. K. Sanderson maintains that Darwin's theory of natural selection is "the most successful theoretical concept ever developed in the entire history of human thought" (2001:332), and Susan Blakemore's admiration is equally fervent:

Darwin's theory of evolution by natural selection is, to my mind, the most beautiful in all of science. It is beautiful because it is so simple and yet its results are so complex. It is counter-intuitive and hard to understand but once you have seen it the world is transformed before your eyes. There is no longer any need for a grand designer to explain all the complexity of the living world. There is just a stark and mindless procedure by which we have all come about—beautiful but scary (1999:10).

The basic idea of natural selection is certainly simple, which is a major source of its appeal, but simplicity alone, unfortunately, is no indication that laws of nature are likely to be correct. As Bertrand Russell observed, "…there can be no *a priori* reason for expecting [natural] laws to be simple except benevolence on the part of Providence towards men of science" (1948:497), and the craving for simplicity actually goes hand in hand with dogmatism and the ability to ignore inconvenient facts. Universal Darwinism is indeed something of a cult of True Believers. Professor Ingold, for example, remarks that "I have found neo-Darwinian selectionists peculiarly intolerant of any intellectual challenge to their point of view. They simply assume it to be unassailable and refuse to discuss it further. Their favourite ploy, of course, is to brand anyone who doesn't fall into line as a crypto-Creationist" (Ingold 2000:2). Richard Alexander gives a good example of this mentality when he claims that inclusive fitness theory is "the *only* [my emphasis] theoretical base from which to undertake a truly comprehensive analysis of human activities and tendencies" (1979:xi), and he is also convinced that it is the final truth and will never need revision: "This general view of organic evolution I regard as firmly established; I do not expect any significant part of it to be retracted or altered in the future..." (ibid., 65), an attitude of mind among evolutionary biologists that has attracted the sarcastic comment "Often in error but never in doubt."

I hope to make clear in this little book that we are not really dealing with science here but with dogma based on faith and the craving for simplicity that tries to persuade by a systematic distortion of the facts, or in some cases simple ignorance of them. But this critical assessment of Darwinism will also provide the basis for an alternative theory of social and cultural evolution which emphasises the principles of self-organisation and human selection. The position from which I begin is the logically inescapable one that in order for selection to operate *there must already be something there to be selected*, so the fundamental question must be how things *originate*, how they are *produced* or *constructed* in the first place. The Darwinist might respond that whatever exists must itself already have passed through a process of selection, but there is no "must" about it. We know that in the inorganic world, such as the evolution of the galaxies, stars, planets, and solar systems (Rees 1998), the weather systems and geology of planets, and the table of elements, sub-atomic structures, and crystalline forms, the operation of physical laws on simple interactions produces more complex forms of order in which selection can have played no part. For example, snowflakes are not hexagonal because this gives them some adaptive advantage.

Amino acids, the building blocks of proteins, were originally self-organised as well, and the first replicating particles of living matter must also have been the product of self-organisation, so it seems rather unlikely that it then simply ceased to operate throughout the rest of biological evolution, and indeed mathematical biologists are finding more and more examples of ordered structures in organisms that are spontaneously generated (e.g. Stewart 2011, Wagner 2014). Self-organisation, in fact, appears to be a pervasive aspect of the whole universe, so that the existence of order cannot as such be attributed to selection without proof, and is an essential aspect of cultural evolution as well.

Since human beings, unlike cells or genes, have consciousness and free will, a huge amount of our technology, institutions, values, and practices are clearly the result of human selection, and in this respect are quite unlike the unconscious biological products of natural selection. On the other hand, while it is obvious that conscious human purposes are constantly at work in every society, the law of unintended consequences is constantly at work as well. While each individual has consciousness, free will and purpose, when two or more individuals are interacting, the relationships between them can also develop in uncontrollable or unpredictable ways that have their own patterns, and which we call self-organisation. One simple example of these sorts of interactions are cycles of vengeance.

Social relationships more generally form complex systems such as the economy that are not under anyone's control or even ability to understand, because self-organisation is an integral part of their formation. The British Constitution is another complex system that is the product of a mass of individual choices, but which interact through self-organisation in unpredictable ways, and the anthropologist studying an unknown tribe soon discovers that their culture has a structure, just as their language will have a grammar. Institutions and belief systems therefore possess structural properties that are as objective as those of the material world, such as the mathematical properties of electoral systems, and which cannot be reduced to the purposes and motives of individuals. Again, it can easily be shown that some institutions will not fit with others, or can be elaborated in certain directions and not in others. In the same way, belief and value systems have a structure which will be more compatible with some institutions and modes of social behaviour than others, and will develop in some directions more easily than in others.

They may also develop in dysfunctional directions. Sometimes this is because systems can work in unintended ways, but also individuals and groups are not like the cells of an organism and rigidly controlled by the genes, but are free to pursue their own interests, so it is not surprising that these interests may clash and social conflict and dysfunction should be normal, while institutions and belief systems themselves may be dysfunctional. This is especially possible because, whereas biological organisms are subject to the stringent requirements of physics and chemistry, so that the mutation of a single gene can be lethal, social and cultural structures can display remarkable disorder and conflict and yet survive indefinitely. So to sum up the differences between cultures and physical organisms we can say that, while self-organisation is a feature of both:

1. Cultures are not physical entities at all, since their individual members are linked by conceptual bonds, not by those of a purely physical nature, and so can *tolerate high levels of dysfunction that would lead to the death of physical organisms.*

2. The individual members of a society, unlike cells or genes, are *capable of acting with purpose and foresight,* learning from experience, and pursuing their own interests, which may also be antisocial.

3. *Human, not natural, selection is responsible for most of a society's adaptive features.*

4. Societies do not reproduce, so there is no obvious reason why *cultural continuity from generation to generation should resemble biological inheritance.*

5. *Cultural variation and selection are linked, so that the random mutation of genes is an entirely inappropriate model of cultural change.*

6. *The biological distinction between ontogeny*—the development of the organism—*and phylogeny*—the development of the species—*does not apply to society,* since societies are capable of radical change to a degree only found in phylogeny, such as when a monarchy transforms into a republic.

So it is not immediately obvious why a Darwinist, surveying these major differences between cultures and organisms, should assume that natural selection would be a promising way of explaining cultural evolution.

2. The Darwinian model

Nevertheless, Dawkins (1978), Lumsden & Wilson 1981, Dennett (1995), Blakemore (1999), Richerson & Boyd (1985, 2006), Mesoudi, Whiten, & Laland (2004), Mesoudi (2016) and many others[1] insist that the evolution of human culture can be explained by natural selection because it has the key features of Darwinian evolution. These are *variation, competition, selection, adaptation,* and *inheritance,* leading to *the accumulation of successful modifications over time.* These concepts form a tightly integrated logical system: *variation* is essential for evolution, because only when there are two or more variant forms can there be *competition,* which itself drives the process of *selection* to find the best *adapted* of the variants, so that evolution proceeds by the accumulation of *inherited* successful adaptations over time:

> ...*cultural evolution is Darwinian, in that it comprises the three general principles of variation, differential fitness and inheritance as laid out by Darwin in* The Origin, *but it is not neo-Darwinian, in that it may not necessarily exhibit the specific mechanisms of genetic inheritance, random mutation etc. that biologists subsequent to Darwin discovered and that were integrated into evolutionary theory during the evolutionary synthesis (Mesoudi 2016:484).*

But it doesn't follow in any way that these "key features" will necessarily combine to work together in the same way in human culture as they are said to do in the case of biological evolution. In particular, the belief that cultural evolution can be explained by *natural* selection rather than human selection is fundamentally confused, as we shall see. The claim that Darwinian principles can explain cultural evolution may have a superficial plausibility but this is only because all these features were originally borrowed from social life in the first place, and in particular, have an obvious resemblance to Adam Smith's free-market capitalism. As Bertrand Russell commented: "From the historical point of view, what is interesting is Darwin's extension to the whole of life of the economics that characterised the philosophical radicals. The motive force of evolution, according to him, is a kind of biological economics in a world of free competition" (1955:755). So of course economists can talk about "competition", "the survival of the fittest", "a Darwinian struggle", and so on, and it is also obvious that all sorts of institutions, artefacts, and ideas appear and disappear over time just as species do, but that does not prove in any way that Darwinism has to be the explanation.

However the version of Darwinism that many Selectionists are trying to apply to cultural evolution is not only based on natural selection but includes the so-called "neo-Darwinian" evolutionary model, which incorporates genetics and developed in the twentieth century. This is the model that actually concerns us, but the arguments against it will also apply to the original version of Darwinism that Mesoudi describes. Darwin knew nothing of genes and believed in the inheritance of acquired characteristics, which allowed the possibility of organisms responding directly to the environment, and these responses becoming part of their heredity. But the eminent nineteenth-century German biologist August Weismann strongly disagreed, and held that information could only pass from what he called the "germ-plasm" (the gonads or sex-organs) to the rest of the body, the "soma", and never vice versa from soma to germ-plasm, and a version of the "Weismann barrier" was later incorporated into twentieth century genetics[2] as part of the neo-Darwinian synthesis. This in itself was a profound change because it denied any interaction between genes and environment, so that *all* variation now had to be thought of as the result of random or blind genetic mutation. These variations then had to be filtered by selection and only those variations that provided an adaptive advantage would be inherited. Evolutionary theory was therefore inevitably forced to *concentrate on finding adaptive reasons* for the survival of every trait, while the *origins* of those traits could be ignored as "random" or "blind" and therefore of no theoretical interest.

The next addition to Darwin's model was a new unit of selection. Darwin had assumed that the individual organism was the unit of selection, and indeed that in some cases the group could also be, if, for example, there was more co-operation between the members of one group than among the members of other competing groups. In modern neo-Darwinian evolutionary biology, however, the orthodox view has developed that selection cannot operate at the level of the group, or even at the level of the individual, but only at the level of the gene. As Dawkins explains:

The central idea I shall make use of was foreshadowed by A. Weismann in pre-gene days at the turn of the century—his doctrine of the "continuity of the germ plasm". I shall argue that the fundamental unit of selection, and therefore of self-interest, is not the species, nor the group, nor even, strictly, the individual. It is the gene, the unit of heredity (Dawkins 1978:12).

Sexual reproduction has the effect of mixing and shuffling genes. This means that any one individual body is just a temporary vehicle for a short-lived combination of genes. The combination of genes which is any one individual may be short-lived, but the genes themselves are potentially very long-lived. Their paths constantly cross and re-cross down the generations. One gene may be regarded as a unit which survives through a number of successive individual bodies (Dawkins 1978:26).

But this introduces the third major variation to the original Darwinian model. Now that the unit of selection is the gene, not the organism, evolutionary development has to be thought of in terms of the *gene pool,* which is all the genes and their variants, or alleles, of a particular *group* of organisms, and selection operates by *changing the relative frequencies of different types of gene in the gene pool* over time. The modern Darwinian conception of evolutionary development is therefore not organic but essentially *populational.* Changes in the design of the organism itself take second place to changes in the relative frequencies of genes in the gene pool, and indeed the organism is now regarded as only a vehicle for the genes. "[Dawkins] urges us to accept the fundamental distinction between 'replicators'—entities whose precise structure is replicated in the process of reproduction—and 'vehicles': entities which are mortal and which are not replicated but whose properties are influenced by replicators" (Corning 2005:464). This has powerful theoretical consequences, making the organism subordinate to the gene and leading to what has become known as "the gene's eye view":

Both biological and cultural evolution involve nothing but [my emphasis] the differential propagation of instructions: soma and

society are merely an instruction's way to make more instructions.
They [soma and society] are epiphenomena. Evolution is not about
the survival of the individual carrier of an instruction; it is about
instructions competing with each other to increase their (respective)
frequencies (Barkow 1978:11).

Or, as it has been put, "A chicken is an egg's way of making another egg". It is for biologists to decide if this is an adequate account of the evolution of plants and animals. My only concern as an anthropologist is to establish if it is an adequate account of cultural evolution and, in particular, if it is true that: "Population thinking is the key to building a causal account of cultural evolution…In the same way that evolutionary theory explains why some genes persist and spread, a sensible theory of cultural evolution will have to explain why some beliefs and attitudes spread and persist while others disappear" (Richerson & Boyd 2006:6).

Going back to the differences between organisms and societies that we noted earlier, it is now clear that all those structural and systemic features that are fundamental to societies have been ignored and simply made to disappear:

The easiest way to make society disappear is simply to dissolve it
by definitional fiat into a mere population.… E. O. Wilson, for
example, writes: "When societies are viewed strictly as populations,
the relationship between culture and heredity can be defined more
precisely". Robert Boyd and Peter Richerson state rather categorically
that "cultural evolution, like genetic evolution in a sexual species,
is always a group or population problem"; and in a later work:
"because cultural change is a population process, it can be studied
using Darwinian methods" (Fracchia & Lewontin 1999:69).

Before we go into the details of the neo-Darwinian theory of cultural evolution one or two preliminary remarks are called for. First of all, the requirement that we have to treat the appearance of novelty as blind or random is extremely strange, an intellectual ball-and-chain around any rational explanation of cultural evolution, since we can usually give a good explanation of how novel variants have appeared. Moreover, Darwin himself never claimed that variation was random. What he actually said was "I have hitherto sometimes spoken as if the variations … had been due to chance. This, of course, is a wholly incorrect expression, but it serves to acknowledge our ignorance of the cause of each particular variation" (1902:98–9). He also believed as we have seen that the experiences of the organism, such as the use of a particular organ, could become hereditary, "the inheritance of acquired characteristics", which is essentially an interactive model between heredity and experience that takes some of the emphasis off selection. Indeed, he didn't even believe that natural selection was the only evolutionary force: "…I am convinced that Natural Selection has been the most important but not the exclusive, means of modification" (ibid., 4), and he often refers to what he calls "the laws of growth"; for example, "We thus see that with plants many morphological changes may be attributed to the laws of growth, and the interaction of parts, independently of natural selection…" (ibid., 163).

Darwin's own views were therefore distinctly more moderate and reasonable than those claimed for him by the advocates of Universal Darwinism, and in any case, how likely is it that a naturalist working in the first half of the nineteenth-century, before the discovery of genetics, and before a century and a half of intense biological research, would have been able to discover a law of nature that could explain all the order in biology, culture, and psychology, or perhaps even in the physical universe as a whole, a law that could be seriously described as "the most successful theoretical concept ever developed in the entire history of human thought"? Since "… the list of things [Darwin] didn't know is practically an encyclopedia of modern biology" (Wagner 2014:33), the answer to my question is, therefore, "Not very likely at all". We are now ready to begin our dissection of the neo-Darwinian theory of cultural evolution, concentrating on the meme, competition and selection, mutation and innovation, and adaptation.

3. The meme and the meme pool

The key move in the replacement of the structural, systemic model of culture by the populational model is the idea that cultures are made up of small components which Dawkins has called memes, analogous to genes, and whose relative frequencies will change in the course of evolution. It is obvious and trivial that over time some cultural traits spread and persist while others disappear, but what is not trivial is the claim that there is a close cultural equivalent of the gene, the meme, and whose essential feature is that like the gene it is capable of replication. Dawkins defines a replicator as having "the extraordinary property of being able to *make copies of itself*" [my emphasis] (1978:16), by which of course he especially has in mind the gene, and then introduces us to the meme, the hypothetical particle of culture which is like the gene because it is also said to be a "replicator":

> *I think that a new kind of replicator has recently emerged on this very planet. It is staring us in the face. It is still in its infancy, still drifting clumsily about in its primeval soup, but already it is achieving evolutionary change at a rate that leaves the old gene panting far behind. The new soup is the soup of human culture. We need a name for the new replicator, a noun that conveys the idea of a unit of cultural transmission, or a unit of imitation. "Mimeme" comes from a suitable Greek root, but I want a monosyllable that sounds a bit like "gene". I hope my classicist friends will forgive me if I abbreviate mimeme to meme.... Examples of memes are tunes, ideas, catchphrases, clothes fashions, ways of making pots or of building arches. Just as genes propagate themselves in the gene pool by leaping from body to body via sperms or eggs, so memes propagate themselves in the meme pool by leaping from brain to brain via a process which, in the broad sense, can be called imitation. If a scientist hears, or reads*

about, a good idea, he passes it on to his colleagues and students. He mentions it in his articles and lectures. If the idea catches on, it can be said to propagate itself, spreading from brain to brain (1978:249).

There is a jumble of metaphorical confusions here which we must now try to disentangle. It does indeed seem that the original replicators must have been free-floating molecules in the primeval soup when life began. But the gene as it exists now is *not* like those free-floating molecules, but is simply a string of DNA that, through an extremely complex cellular process, produces a protein, and which after even more complex processes reappears in sperm cells or eggs. In other words, as Dawkins of course knows perfectly well, genes do not propagate themselves by leaping from body to body since they can only be replicated by the cells of the organism of which they are part: they are not replica*tors* but replicat*ed*, which is a fundamental difference. Secondly, the genes of an organism collectively make up its "genotype", which then gets "translated" by an extraordinarily complex process into the "phenotype", the trillions of specialised cells which make up flesh, blood, bone and the rest of the bodily organs. But in cultures there is no equivalent to the genotype/phenotype distinction, a fundamental point to which we shall return in a moment.

How does the meme fit into all of this? First of all, an idea or cultural variant obviously does *not* propagate itself or "leap from brain to brain" as Dawkins so bizarrely describes it. I say bizarre because ideas clearly cannot have an independent existence like viruses: Dawkins himself admits that *we* do all the propagating, and that it is the scientist, in this case, who is obviously spreading the various memes from brain to brain in his articles and lectures. Nor, when we learn a new idea can it be described as parasitizing us—it is *we* who accept or reject *it.* There is also the same basic confusion in his notion of the meme as replicator as in his notion of the gene. He has defined a replicator as having "the extraordinary property of being able to *make copies of itself*" but he defines the meme in the passage quoted above as "a unit of cultural transmission, or a unit of *imitation*" [original emphasis] (ibid., 206)[3]. The ability of any entity to make copies of itself is indeed extraordinary, but a unit of imitation or transmission can't make copies of itself, almost by definition. Being imitated or copied or transmitted is a purely passive process, since the process of copying is in the hands of an extraneous agent like a body or a human being. The letter A, for example, in a text is merely a unit of imitation, whereas to become a self-replicator it would have to be equipped, perhaps in a computer programme, with a set of instructions about how to draw itself as well, a self-replication or self-assembly code.

And we return again to that fundamental point I raised earlier, that "the good idea" which Dawkins talks about, and his tunes, ways of making pots and so on are totally unlike the gene, because they remain themselves; they do not "code" for something else, like a gene coding for a protein, because in cultures that distinction between the genotype and the phenotype of an organism simply doesn't exist. This is a crucial point which is enough by itself to invalidate the whole concept of the meme as analogous to the gene.

We next have to define what exactly are going to count as memes. A gene is straightforwardly defined as a sequence of DNA that codes for a protein, and specific genes are regularly isolated, silenced, transferred and so on by experimenters and in various forms of genetic modification. But how to define a meme, however, has been a persistent and fundamental problem ever since the idea was first proposed. Dawkins's "tunes, ideas, catch-phrases, clothes fashions, ways of making pots or of building arches", or Lumsden's and Wilson's "food items, colour classifications, 6000 attributes of camels among Arabs, and the ten-second-slow-downs by drivers which cause traffic-jams" do not inspire much confidence that we have discovered here a powerful new scientific concept that will provide a unique insight into human culture. So some Darwinians have therefore suggested that it is not really necessary to think of memes as small *precise* units:

Many people believe that a Darwinian approach to cultural evo-lution requires breaking culture into little, independent bits, an anathema to many anthropologists who believe that cultures are tightly integrated systems of shared meanings….[B]ut there is ab-solutely nothing in the theory that requires that cultural variants be little bits of culture. People may choose between great, linked cultural complexes—between speaking Spanish or Guarani, or be-tween remaining a Catholic or becoming a Seventh Day Adventist, or they may choose between smaller, more loosely linked items of knowledge—between pronouncing r *at the end of a word or not, or between different views about the morality of contraception. At a* formal *level, Darwinian methods will apply equally well in either case (Richerson & Boyd 2006:90–91).*

Again, Dennett, having reminded us that Darwinian evolution "de-pends on *very* high fidelity copying" of the DNA, then goes on to say:

Minds (or brains) on the other hand, aren't much like photocopying machines at all. On the contrary, instead of just dutifully passing on their messages, correcting most of the typos as they go, brains seem to be designed to do just the opposite: to transform, invent, interpolate, censor, and generally mix up the "input" before yielding any "output". Isn't one of the hallmarks of cultural evolution and transmission the extraordinarily high rate of mutation and recombination? (Dennett 1995:355).

Like Richerson and Boyd he is unhappy with the degree of precision required of the meme, and instead argues that the meme should be thought of as the "distinctly memorable unit": "One of the most strik-ing features of cultural evolution is the ease, reliability, and confidence with which we can identify commonalities in spite of vast differences in underlying media" (ibid., 356). He mentions the common theme in the plots of *Romeo and Juliet* and *West Side Story*, pottery styles, monarchy, and tattooing, and on p.344 gives the examples of the

Odyssey, calculus, chess, perspective drawing, and evolution by natural selection as "memorable units". The search for the meme is clearly going nowhere, because a meme can be anything at all to which one can put a name, so these jumbles of bits and pieces cannot possibly form a population, or comprise a meme pool analogous to a gene pool.

A gene pool is a genuine example of a statistical population, which is a data set of related, discrete items that can be compared in order to answer some question or to be used in an experiment. In a given population of peppered moths, for example, we may ask what are the relative percentages of genes for light colour and for dark. By contrast, a meme pool is not a statistical population at all but a more or less infinite jumble of bits and pieces of anything one can think of and whose relative frequencies are therefore meaningless—as in comparing the sales of strawberry ice-creams with the sales of Sir Walter Scott's novels. Dawkins himself describes the meme pool as soup: "…in general memes resemble the early replicating molecules, floating chaotically free in the primeval soup, rather than modern genes in their neatly paired chromosomal regiments" (ibid., 211), or again, the meme is "still drifting clumsily about in its primeval soup,… the soup of human culture" (ibid., 206).

But "the soup of human culture" has to be a real living culture of actual people doing things, not just a list of traits, and whatever culture may be it has absolutely no resemblance to soup. The words, ideas, artefacts, and so on that constitute Dawkins's "cultural soup" can do nothing on their own account: *we* have to produce them and communicate them, and we do so in the course of highly structured and complex activities, like writing books such as *The Selfish Gene*, in which the "memes" are chosen by the author in relation to their appropriateness to the topics under discussion, the author's purposes, the rules of grammar, and so on.

Now of course it is true that in order to participate in a culture its individual members have to store large numbers of pieces of information in their brains. But higher order principles are constantly imparting a structure to these pieces of information. The rules of grammar structure the words in our sentences, and the rules of our culture organise the various items that we learn. For example, as they grow up, members of all societies have to learn and remember words like "mother", "father", "brother", and "sister", but these words are not just isolated bits of information—like, perhaps, the names of flowers—but are the connected parts of a cultural system of social categories and roles: a mother is also a wife, and a wife has a husband, who is the father of their children, who are brothers and sisters, and their mother's brother's children and father's sister's children are different types of cousin (matrilateral and patrilateral cross-cousins) because their parents' siblings are of opposite sexes. Children of father's brothers and mother's sisters, on the other hand, are parallel cousins, for whom there may be different marriage rules from cross-cousins. People may be expected to marry their matrilateral, but not their patrilateral cross-cousins, and will have different duties to their non-lineal and their lineal relatives, and to their in-laws, for example, and all these roles will be governed by a variety of norms such as respect, sharing, shame, and avoidance. The other members of the society have the same mental map of the kinship and marriage system, so that they are all actors within the constraints and opportunities of what we may call the same social landscape.

A few minutes' thought should show anyone that it is totally inappropriate to represent organised systems—societies, knowledge structures, languages, machines, bodies, and so on—simply as *populations* of bits and pieces, meme-soup, because counting the relative frequencies of the "memes" can tell us nothing about their different functions within these systems. In a hierarchical organisation, for example, the topmost positions are necessarily less numerous than the lower positions, so generals are much rarer than privates, but what would it mean to say that they had less "fitness"? Monarchy, with only one living representative at any one time, may outlast whole classes such as monks or samurai because of the importance in the social structure of the monarchical institution. There are also many specialised roles that involve relatively few people but are nevertheless essential for the functioning of the society, just as there are many examples of rare but essential bits of technology, and so on.

The idea of the meme as an active agent also makes as much nonsense out of our minds as it does out of culture. Just as our bodies are said to be nothing more than vehicles which genes use to perpetuate themselves, so our minds are supposed to be mere vehicles which memes parasitize to perpetuate themselves as well. The mind, in this view, then, is a purely passive receptacle for the thoughts represented in memes, whose competitive jostlings throughout human history have resulted in the emergence of modern culture, science, and technology, and the political and economic institutions through which they operate. This "mind as vehicle" perspective can therefore have no room at all for the notion of cognitive development, in which the mind is not a passive vehicle which is simply being constantly loaded up with memes, but plays the central role in the selection and generation of memes. Memeticists are effectively asking us to believe, for example, that the historical development of mathematics from tribal concepts limited to "single" and "pair", through Babylonian and Greek mathematics, to the immense flourishing of mathematics in modern civilisation, has not involved any development of human cognitive abilities but is simply the result of the natural selection of memes over the generations. (I am not alluding here to any genetic changes, but simply to the development of new cognitive skills in the context of new social and cultural environments.) Memetics, in short, has nothing to say about the very obvious facts of cognitive development in human history, and which we will investigate further in Chapter IV.

Finally, one must also point out that the notion of the brain as nothing more than the passive vehicle for an active population of competing memes that parasitize it is ultimately self-refuting. According to Susan Blakemore, "Our capacity to think and solve problems is designed to give true rather than false answers, so in general, true memes should thrive better than false ones" (Blakemore 1999:180). But in fact a vast amount of human thought is mistaken, at least to some degree, and since Blakemore is particularly keen to combat "false" memes, notably those of religion and the "illusion" of personal identity, she is obliged to admit that "Memes do not need to be true to be successful" (ibid., 180). She concedes that it is to the memes' advantage to be able to mimic truth, just as it is to their advantage to be able to mimic altruism, and other desirable memes like "successful", "scientific", "supported by overwhelming evidence", "a triumphant paradigm", and so on. Since the only "aim" of memes is to replicate as much as possible, there is no reason why they should have any innate bias towards truth or anything else of concern to human beings. Remember that "The first rule of memes, as for genes, is that replication is not necessarily for the good of anything; replicators flourish that are good at … replication— for whatever reason!" (Dennett 1995:362).

So how can we tell when memes are only mimicking the truth? Blakemore has ruled out the operation of conscious reasoning as a means to attain truth, so there can only be the mindless competition of the memes inside the "meme habitat" of our brains, and since we cannot expect the memes themselves to be honest with us there seems no way left by which any objective notion of truth could be established. Memes can only be more or less *successful*, then, not more or less *true*, from which it follows that memetics itself is only one memeplex among hosts of others, and like the rest of human knowledge can have no claim to objective truth. So Dennett's "universal acid" dissolves the whole of science and mathematics, with all other forms of truth, and instead of "a revolutionised world-view" merely leaves universal nonsense.

I think it can be said that we have allowed the meme a fair gallop round the course, but it seems to have fallen at every fence. So it's hardly surprising, then, that although it has now been around for more than forty years, staggering (metaphorically) like a zombie from one learned publication to another, no one has ever been able to show that it can actually solve any problems or explain any puzzles. The contrast with the gene could hardly be more extreme.

4. Competition and selection

If all that one means by "selection" is success or failure, survival or disappearance, then there are obviously plenty of cultural examples, as there are in the case of plants and animals, but in neo-Darwinian theory the idea of natural selection is a good deal more specific than this. In explaining what he meant by natural selection in the *Origin*, Darwin first discussed human selection by plant and animal breeders:

We cannot suppose that all the breeds were suddenly produced as perfect and useful as we now see them; indeed, in many cases we know that this has not been their history. The key is man's power of accumulative selection; nature gives successive variations; man adds them up in a certain direction useful to him. In this sense he may be said to have made himself useful breeds. (Origin, 21.)...[For example] No doubt the strawberry had always varied since it was cultivated, but the slight varieties had always been neglected. As soon, however, as gardeners picked out individual plants with slightly larger, earlier, or better fruit, and raised seedlings from them, and again picked out the best seedlings and bred from them, then ... those many admirable varieties of the strawberry were raised which have appeared during the last half-century (Origin, 28).

In the wild state, however, where there are no gardeners or animal breeders, plants and animals are instead engaged in a struggle for survival:

A struggle for existence inevitably follows from the high rate at which all beings tend to increase. Every being, which during its natural lifetime produces several eggs or seeds, must suffer destruction during some period of its life, and during some season or occasional year, otherwise, on the principle of geometrical increase, its number would quickly become so inordinately great that no country could support the product. Hence, as more individuals are produced than can possibly survive, there must in every case be a struggle for existence, either one individual with another of the same species, or with the individuals of distinct species, or with the physical conditions of life. It is the doctrine of Malthus applied with manifold force to the whole vegetable and animal kingdoms; for in this case there can be no artificial increase of food, and no prudential restraint from marriage (ibid., 46–7).

Darwin was very clear that this Malthusian principle was the foundation of his whole theory:

Nothing is easier than to admit in words the truth of the universal struggle for life, or more difficult—at least I have found it so—than constantly to bear this conclusion in mind. But unless it be thoroughly engrained in the mind, the whole economy of nature, with every fact on distribution, rarity, abundance, extinction, and variation, will be dimly seen or quite misunderstood (ibid., 46).

Now it was essential for Darwin to introduce the idea of a struggle for existence because without it there could be nothing to drive the weeding-out of inferior variants similar to that practised by plant and animal breeders, a process which he called "Natural Selection":

Owing to this struggle, variations, however slight, and from whatever cause proceeding, if they be in any degree profitable to the individuals of a species ... will tend to the preservation of such individuals, and will generally be inherited by the offspring.... I have called this principle, by which each slight variation, if useful, is preserved, by the term Natural Selection, in order to mark its relation to man's power of selection. But the expression often used by Mr Herbert Spencer of the Survival of the Fittest is more accurate, and is sometimes equally convenient (ibid., 45).

It is more accurate, of course, first of all because "survival" envisages the possibility of "failure", where an organism simply collapses from internal defects, regardless of any competition, and there are plenty of social analogues for this. Perhaps more importantly it avoids the metaphor of "selection", with its implication that Nature can have conscious purposes. On this Darwin comments: "In the literal sense of the word, no doubt, natural selection is a false term,… but who objects to an author speaking of the attraction of gravity as ruling the movements of the planets? Everyone knows what is meant and implied by such metaphorical expressions; and they are almost necessary for brevity" (ibid., 58).

Nevertheless, metaphors can take on a life of their own, and this particular metaphor is confusing because "selection" inevitably suggests purpose and agency, and therefore seems to have encouraged people to treat natural selection as if it could include human selection. As we shall see in a moment, this certainly confused Darwin himself. So it is not surprising that according to Richerson and Boyd, "The logic of natural selection applies to culturally transmitted variation every bit as much as it applies to genetic variation" (2006:76). In their view, the "logic of natural selection" means (a) people vary in their beliefs (like variant genes); (b) some beliefs increase the probability that individuals will transmit them to others (like having more offspring); (c) and there is a limit to the number of beliefs or cultural variants in a population so *that cultural variants must compete*, thereby increasing or decreasing their frequency. This is an essential point, but just how are memes or cultural variants supposed to compete in the struggle for life? According to Dawkins:

Any user of a digital computer knows how precious computer time and memory storage space are [written back in 1976].... The computers in which memes live are human brains. Time is possibly a more important limiting factor than storage space, and it is the subject of heavy competition. The human brain, and the body which

*it controls, cannot do more than one or a few things at once. If a
meme is to dominate the attention of a human brain, it must do so at
the expense of "rival" memes. Other commodities for which memes
compete are radio and television time, billboard space, newspaper
column inches, and library shelf-space (Dawkins 1978:211–12).*

This is exceptionally feeble. The human memory is extraordinary,
and the fact that we can only concentrate on one meme at a time
obviously doesn't stop us thinking about all sorts of other memes a
few moments later, while memes have never been more widely spread
around than through the limitless facilities of our modern forms of
mass communication. Mesoudi *et al.* (2004) do a rather better job
of answering this question, which was raised because Darwin in *The
Descent of Man* (1871) had become fascinated by languages as analogous to species, and they quote Darwin himself on linguistic competition (although *he* was actually quoting Max Müller): "A struggle
for life is constantly going on amongst the words and grammatical
forms in each language. The better, the shorter, the easier forms
are constantly gaining the upper hand, and they owe their success to
their own inherent virtue" (from *The Descent of Man*, p.91). They
continue:

*Clearly, the "struggle" Darwin was alluding to here cannot be directly
compared to the competition over finite physical resources alluded to
by the reference to Malthus. Rather, we have to think in more general
terms, of a competition for limited "slots" or functionally equivalent
"solutions" to specific "problems".… We suggest that an appropriate
way to conceptualise what any set of cultural variations are in general
competing over is in terms of functional categories. Thus, synonyms
will be in competition for describing the same semantic category;
different hammers will be in competition for effective hammering;
and different gestures may be in competition to fulfil the same social
function (2004:4).*

By 1871 when *The Descent of Man* was published Darwin seems to have forgotten what he had written in the *Origin* about human selection, because he adds with approval, "The survival or preservation of certain favoured words in the struggle for existence is natural selection". But how exactly, one might ask Darwin, do "better, shorter, easier words" differ from "slightly larger, earlier, or better" strawberry plants, whose selection by growers was supposed in the *Origin* to be an example of human selection, and the exact *opposite* of natural selection? Darwin here is hopelessly confused, as are all the Selectionists who have followed him. The whole passage quoted above is in fact a nonsensical piece of self-mystification: words and grammatical forms and all the other "memes" or cultural variants can't struggle with each other, least of all for life, or "gain the upper hand", for two simple reasons. First, they aren't alive. And second, the so-called "struggle" *is actually taking place inside our own minds, not in the physical world outside.* I will explain.

Two boxers in the ring are certainly competing and struggling with each other for a limited slot, and trying to gain the upper hand. But if in writing a sentence I am trying to decide whether to use the synonyms "victory" or "success" in what sense are these words competing like boxers with each other for "a limited slot"? Quite obviously they are not competitors at all because, unlike the boxers, they can't *do* anything themselves, and have only been brought together in my imagination. The reality is that I am having to make a choice, a selection, and it is *my* internal mental conflict that is being metaphorically transformed into a competition between the two words. Again, if we have to pack a small travel bag with essentials, do our hair-brushes and our shaving kit have to compete with each other against our pyjamas and our sponge-bag to get into it, or do *we* simply have to be more rigorous than usual in *our own choices* of what to pack? All these alleged competitors are in fact the passive objects of our choice, of our own human selection, not of natural selection at all. *The delusion that cultural variants or memes are active agents like plants and animals*

*that can compete with one another in a struggle for existence, and that
the result of this competition is decided by natural selection, is at the very
heart of the Selectionist model but is really nothing more than metaphorical
nonsense.*

We can, however, say that certain areas of life such as business, scientific research, or the law are highly competitive, meaning that the *people* in them deal with many cultural variants, but subject them to a stringent process of selection in argumentative competition with one another. The opposite conditions of low competition would be where there is only one way of doing something, or, where there are several variants but they will all work after a fashion, and it doesn't really matter which gets chosen. I call this "the survival of the mediocre"; it is very widespread in our society and especially in primitive society, and we shall discuss it in more detail when we come to the problems of adaptation.

There are also many cultural variants or "memes" whose increases it would be very strange to describe as the results of any kind of selection just on the grounds that they have become more frequent, such as increases in unemployment, the frequency of traffic-jams, or bankruptcies. These could reasonably be considered as maladaptive "memes", but it might seem just as strange to call them the results of natural selection as it would be to say they were the direct results of human choice. What we actually have here is not "natural selection" at all but social *processes*, involving some human selection (like choosing to drive on a congested highway) together with self-organisation, that together *produce* certain negative consequences over which no one has full control.

5. Mutation and cultural innovation

At this point we have to remind ourselves that the whole Selectionist model of culture is essentially static, a *pool* of memes or cultural variants whose components do not interact with each other but simply change over time, whereas of course it is also a mass of complex *processes,* and processes involve events. These can obviously have a strong element of the accidental and the random about them but still have very powerful effects on the rest of the culture—wars, revolutions, technological discoveries, disasters, and so on. Accidental events, then, are a prominent feature of human culture, but human purpose is also responsible for a huge range of innovations in everything from technology to the arts to social institutions, and the question is therefore how this is to be squared with the Darwinian emphasis on random mutation.

Here we must remember that random innovation is absolutely essential to the neo-Darwinian programme because it is the justification for claiming that selection is the all-powerful source of order, "a scheme for creating Design out of Chaos without the aid of Mind". If Selectionists were to admit that human purpose is a very powerful factor in cultural innovation they would therefore have to concede that selection could not have the universal power that they claim for it. So while it may seem obvious that a great deal of cultural innovation is conscious and purposeful and not random at all, this has been rejected by Darwinists on the grounds that being conscious and purposeful is no guarantee that the new variation will actually work:

> *We might speculate, however, that whatever the good faith and insight of the proponents of innovations of any kind, the chance that the innovations will prove truly adaptive in the long run is not 100%, so that many innovations, however purposeful and intelligent they may seem to their proponents and first adopters, may not turn out to be highly adaptive, at least on a long term basis. Because of this, and because some cultural mutation is simply copy error, a significant proportion of new cultural mutations might be truly random without any semblance of adaptiveness (Cavalli-Sforza and Feldman 1981:65–6).*

Mesoudi similarly argues that "Critics of Darwinian cultural evolution frequently assert that whereas biological evolution is blind and undirected, cultural change is directed or guided by people who possess foresight, thereby invalidating any Darwinian analysis of culture" (Mesoudi 2008:243). He objects to this because it assumes that "human foresight is highly accurate, reliable, and influential, for which there is little empirical support" (ibid., 245). These objections, however, are entirely beside the point because no one is claiming that all innovations have to be adaptive, or achieve their aims, only that even if they don't they can still have a significant cultural impact, just as accidents and disasters can. So failure—the disappointment of foresight, in other words—has also been an important factor in cultural evolution and an integral part of human life. This is especially true of modern industrial societies, which are extraordinarily complex, and where most government initiatives go wrong as a matter of course. An excellent British analysis, for example, is *The Blunders of our Governments* (King & Crewe 2013).

Prohibition, for example, seemed to many Americans an obvious remedy against the scourge of drunkenness, and was initially popular, but later was generally admitted to have been a social disaster: it caused serious unemployment among many businesses that had relied on the liquor industry, and the loss of government revenue had serious effects on state and federal finances. Enforcement of Prohibition overwhelmed the law courts, turned millions of normally law-abiding Americans into criminals, led to widespread bribery and corruption of public officials especially the police, and promoted general contempt for the law. One of the most serious consequences was that banning a commodity like alcohol, for which there was an enormous popular demand, created an ideal business opportunity for criminals to exploit, and to expand their activities to an unprecedented degree. Before Prohibition, criminal gangs were mainly local threats, but the need to organise the shipment of vast quantities of illegal alcohol, especially from Canada and the Caribbean, required large-scale logistical co-operation between well-organised gangs prepared to use extreme violence, and whose influence has continued to this day. And because home-made and illicit alcohol was so easily available more Americans began drinking than ever before. Although Prohibition was repealed in 1931, it nevertheless made permanent changes to American society, like many other far more disastrous social decisions and ideologies to other societies throughout history.

It is also of the first importance to remember that in the neo-Darwinian model environmental selection and genetic mutation are unconnected, independent variables, so that what does the selecting is not itself directly affected by what it selects. Cultural innovations, however, are normally made by people who are members of the same culture as those who will do the selecting, and may be the very same people, so that variation and selection are linked aspects of a single system, the common culture, rather like having a discussion with one-self. So Karl Marx, heavily influenced by German idealist philosophy, French socialism, and British economic ideas, and by his experience of the capitalism of the Industrial Revolution, formed the theory that class conflict was the principal driver of cultural evolution. This in turn fed back into European culture and because it was in tune with many of its traditional beliefs, including biblical notions of history, it had a profound effect on subsequent political developments. Innovations are therefore not blind at all, since they may be the product of the same cultural factors upon which their acceptance depends, and we may therefore expect to find a strongly directional quality in cultural evolution for this reason. The proliferation of "human rights" and "identity politics" in modern Western society are good examples.

Again, it is often said that the trial-and-error that is a typical feature of human invention is basically the same as random mutation, but there is a fundamental difference. Random mutation in plants and animals by definition can have no goal or target, but targets are normal in human invention because they guide and give direction to the trials that are made, while a whole range of possible trials are dismissed or not even considered by the inventor because they are irrelevant to what he is trying to achieve.

Trying to account for innovations as the product of random variation is in fact a camouflage for ignorance, as Darwin said, and which excuses us from investigating how the significant innovations in human history have really occurred. While this is much more intellectually demanding than just assuming random or blind variation, it is only this that will show us how things first appear within any society. Investigating the background and circumstances of inventions, revolutions, and new beliefs and practices is in fact the standard procedure of historians, sociologists, economists and everyone else in the humanities and the social sciences. Instead of randomness or accident, we more often find that not only may there be a limited range of options, but that there can be easy gateways into new ideas or discoveries, or that some important change has been made easier by a particular set of conditions that can themselves often be explained.

We do not find, generally speaking, that people try out vast numbers of different ways of doing things, and that the most efficient is ultimately selected by a process of competition, in which inferior variants are eliminated. There is usually only a limited range of choices, and people generally opt for the one that is the easiest or most convenient—it would be very odd if they didn't—but doing what is easiest is the opposite of random. So, for example, just about every verbal number system in the world is based on 10. Are we to believe that this was the result of some trial-and-error process in which thousands of societies tried out all sorts of other numbers, and that only those systems based on ten survived? Or, did people almost always go for ten in the first place, without any trial-and-error, simply because we have ten fingers, and that was the easy and obvious choice?

More generally, people do what is easiest when it is in accordance with human nature, something which so far has not seriously entered the discussion. There is, of course, a long tradition in anthropology of claiming that all human behaviour is dictated by culture, and denying that there is any such thing as human nature, which I regard as an absurd denial of the obvious and contradicted by overwhelming evidence.

We shall go into it in much more detail in Chapter III, and here I will simply point out that in so far as human nature has an effect both on the innovations people introduce, and on their success, then the random element must have so much the less significance in explaining innovation.

If cultural innovations were blind or random like genetic mutations, they would be inexplicable, spontaneous phenomena whose origins were sealed off from everything in the world around them by a version of the Weissman barrier. They are in fact an integral part of social life and, like everything else in it are the combined results of human choice and self-organisation.

6. Adaptation

The central place of selection in the neo-Darwinian scheme of things means of course that the notion of adaptation is absolutely crucial as well because it is the criterion in terms of which selection takes place—well-adapted traits will be selected and poorly adapted traits will not. But despite its apparent simplicity the idea of adaptation has proved to be extremely subtle and challenging. As the leading geneticist Richard Lewontin has said, "There is virtually universal disagreement among students of evolution as to the meaning of adaptation" (1957:395), and G. G. Simpson wrote that "The subject is so intricate that even here no more than a very general and summary statement can be attempted" (1953:160). The problem is that adaptive explanations, in contrast to causal explanations, are inherently feeble (Hallpike 2011c).

This is because traits, whether biological or sociocultural, do not exist in isolation, but as parts of complex systems about whose working we often know only too little, and these systems also have histories, about which we often know even less. In this context of ignorance, the adaptive explanation has to take a short cut, and fall back on the much weaker strategy of trying to see how the particular trait works in its present environment, and in what ways it might be useful. When a use is found it is then claimed to be the explanation of why the trait or feature exists, but this assumes that every trait must have a function (or else it would have been eliminated by selection), and that the function of the trait can be inferred from its form. Neither of these assumptions, however, is necessarily true at all. Form may be a most ambiguous guide to function, and a trait may simply be the result of productive processes and have no use (like the brittleness of cast-iron), or any particular uses or benefits may be quite accidental. It will obviously be difficult, then, even for biologists to distinguish mere "Just So Stories" from genuine adaptive explanations, as G. C. Williams has said:

> *A frequent practice is to recognise adaptation in any recognisable benefit arising from the activities of an organism. I believe that this is an insufficient basis for postulating adaptation and that it has led to some serious errors. A benefit can be the result of chance instead of design. The decision as to the purpose of a mechanism must be based on an examination of the machinery and an argument as to the appropriateness of the means to an end. It cannot be based on value judgements of actual or probable consequences (Williams 1966:12).*

But these difficulties have led to very uncritical uses of the notion of adaptation:

> *I call that approach to evolutionary studies which assumes without further proof that all aspects of the morphology, physiology, and behaviour of organisms are adaptive optimal solutions to problems* the adaptationist programme. *It is not a contingent theory of evolution or hypothesis to be tested since adaptation and optimality are* a priori *assumptions. Rather, it is a program of explanation and exemplification in which the purpose of the investigator is to show* how *organisms solve problems optimally, not to test if they do (Lewontin 1979:6).*

What Lewontin refers to as "the adaptationist programme" has been an almost inevitable feature of neo-Darwinian theory when applied to cultural evolution. But one of the most obvious differences between societies and organisms is that societies are made up of separate people, each with their own points of view, aims, and interests that may frequently conflict, quite unlike the component cells of the biological organism, each of which is assigned its place and role in the organism by the genotype. While, therefore, one can expect that the developmental processes of the organism will normally generate a harmonious and efficient entity, there is much less reason to expect a similar outcome in the case of human societies.

Since societies are maintained by the separate physical individuals who compose them, it is surely quite likely, then, that different kin groups, communities, classes, and factions within a society may pursue courses of action in the interests of their own members which conflict with those of others, and with the efficient working of the whole society. There is therefore no reason in principle why all these individuals should somehow work in concordance so that they produce, unknown to themselves, practices and institutions that are adaptive either for the majority of individuals, or for the working of the whole social system. We know in fact that as societies increase in complexity, harmony is only achieved with great effort, and exploitation, feuding, and criminality may flourish. Efficient government of states, in particular, has proved extraordinarily difficult, because of the problems of administration, of preventing rebellion, and not least, because of the temptations of absolute power for rulers. It was not entirely without reason that Gibbon described history, not as the steady accumulation of increasingly well-adapted institutions, but as "little more than the register of the crimes, follies, and misfortunes of mankind". Indeed, it is extremely hard to understand how *non-purposeful* mechanisms that contributed towards social solidarity could be anything other than accidental.

The existence of different groupings and hierarchical levels of organisation also raises the problem for any proposed adaptive explanation: "adaptive for whom?" In the case of primitive warfare, for example, we may find that it preserves the survival of the inhabitants of particular villages, yet at the same time disturbs the peace of the wider region. Writing of the Yanomamo of South America, Chagnon claims that "a militant ideology and the warfare it entails function to preserve the sovereignty of individual villages in a milieu of chronic warfare" (Chagnon 1967:112). But it is clear:

> ...*that social interaction takes place between a* number *of autonomous villages, and that there are forms of alliance varying from trade, to feasting, the exchange of women and the giving of refuge to allies worsted in battle, and that the villages are all integral parts of a larger social system.... Thus while it can be argued that it is adaptive for any* one *village to engage in warfare, and be generally ferocious, in a situation where everyone else is equally ferocious, it does not follow that it is adaptive for that* group *of villages to engage in constant raiding and feuding among themselves—they would be much better off in terms of material prosperity if they lived at peace (Hallpike 1973:454).*

This multiplicity of organisational levels in human society means that, since one can always find some level for which a practice such as warfare is beneficial, using the notion of adaptation to explain its survival may be quite arbitrary.

But because human beings have obvious needs—for food, shelter, protection from the elements and danger, entertainment, and so on—one is not of course denying that many aspects of culture and social institutions may be useful, or adaptive, because people have deliberately designed them to be so. Human selection of this kind, of course, has nothing to do with natural selection, but the Darwinian emphasis on adaptation has naturally led many to claim that if some social practice or institution is common, then this must have been the result of some special adaptive advantage it possesses, *even if the people themselves are unaware of what this is.* It was especially tempting for anthropologists, faced as they were by what seemed to them the many strange and apparently useless customs of non-literate societies, and where there was little or nothing in the way of historical records to shed light on why these customs might have been adopted.

According to Malinowski, for example, "The functional view of culture insists therefore upon the principle that in every type of civilisation, every custom, material object, idea and belief fulfils some vital function, has some task to accomplish, represents an indispensable part within a working whole" (Malinowski 1926:133). (Compare the identical view of an evolutionary biologist: "On theoretical grounds, all existing features of animals are adaptive. If they were not adaptive, then they would have been eliminated by selection and would disappear" cited by Gould & Vrba 1982:6.) So the adaptive value of warfare in New Guinea has been alleged to be rectifying man-resource imbalances (Vayda 1971); ritual cycles among the Maring maintain the correct size of pig herds (Rappaport 1968); large scale human sacrifice among the Aztecs was really to provide high quality protein from cannibalism (Harris 1980:334–40); the combination of matrilocal residence and patrilineal descent reduces the risk of feuding (Murphy 1957); matrilateral cross-cousin marriage provides more effective social cohesion than patrilateral cross-cousin marriage and is therefore much commoner (Lévi-Strauss 1969:445–6). The cow is sacred in India because of its manure and its value as a draught animal (Harris 1978:141–2). The segmentary lineage has been selected for in tribes that are involved in predatory expansion against their neighbours (Sahlins 1961). Divination by hunters in North America is actually a randomising technique which allows them to find more game than they would by conscious judgement (Moore 1957), and so on. Durkheim expressed an idea that became part of the common stock of anthropological thought:

It would be incomprehensible if the most widespread forms of organisation would not at the same time be, at least in their aggregate, the most advantageous. How could they have maintained themselves under so great a variety of circumstances if they had not enabled the individual better to resist the elements of destruction? On the other hand, the reason for the rarity of the other characteristics is evidently that the average organism possessing them has greater difficulty in surviving. The greater frequency of the former is, thus, a proof of their superiority (Durkheim 1964:58).

This essentially Darwinian assumption underlay the Functionalist school of anthropology for many decades of the twentieth century, and while Functionalism has long ceased to be fashionable its adaptationist philosophy continues to be supported by contemporary evolutionary biologists. A good example of a universal feature of human society alleged to be the consequence of natural selection is the tendency of languages to diversify:

This variability is extremely puzzling given that a universal, un-changing language would seem to be the most useful form of commu-nication. That language has evolved to be parochial, not universal is surely no accident. Security would have been far more important than ease of communication with outsiders. Given the incessant warfare between early human groups, a highly variable language would have served to exclude outsiders and to identify strangers the moment they opened their mouths. Dialects, writes the evolutionary psychologist Robin Dunbar, are "particularly well designed to act as badges of group membership that allow everyone to identify members of their exchange group; dialects are difficult to learn well, generally have to be learned young, and change sufficiently rapidly that it is possible to identify an individual not just within a locality but also within a generation within that locality" (Wade 2007:204).

The fallacies here should be obvious. First of all, an entirely bogus criterion of linguistic usefulness, "a universal, unchanging language", is set up by the Darwinian theorist, who is then puzzled by the ac-tual variability of language from group to group. This multiplicity of dialects therefore becomes a "problem" that has to be explained by its adaptive value, which is that "dialects are particularly well designed to act as badges of group membership". But why would a universal unchanging language necessarily be the most useful, the most adaptive form of communication, in the first place? It all depends on circumstances. A "universal unchanging language" would be very useful in the global society of the modern world, which is why we have English. But primitive societies are small and relatively isolated from one another, certainly by comparison with modern societies, so being able to converse with people one could never meet would have been of no use whatever. How would groups of Aborigines all across Australia, for example, have benefited from being able to talk to one another if they never actually had the chance of meeting in ten thousand years? Secondly, in primitive societies people know the members of their own social group by sight anyway, so if a stranger appears on the scene he is identifiable as such before he even opens his mouth, which would seem to make dialect differences rather redundant. If there is any doubt they can question him about his background—his clan, where he lives— and would easily be able to identify real strangers in this way without any dialect differences.

Finally, there is a simple and obvious causal explanation for the development of different dialects (and of different languages, of course) that has nothing to do with adaptation and selection, and which is known as "drift". Over the generations there is a steady accumulation of accidental variations in the speech patterns of each population, and linguistic diversification between groups is simply the result of the relative *lack of social interaction between them*, and increases in proportion to the length of their mutual isolation from one another. Local divergences of this kind are not, of course, confined to language at all, but occur across the whole spectrum of human behaviour and custom, and are analogous to what biologists refer to as "genetic drift".

Another basic problem with the whole adaptationist approach to cultural evolution is that it assumes the universality of adaptation, and in many cases *optimal* adaptation, without being able to produce any mechanism by which human societies could have regularly achieved this without conscious intention. Biologists trying to explain some physical trait in a species can appeal to natural selection operating on millions of organisms over millions of years, whereas the anthropologist only has a few thousand societies over a few thousand years, and to suppose that maladaptive customs must have been weeded out by a process of natural selection comparable to that of living organisms would require astronomical rates of social change and extinction for which there is not the slightest evidence. Instead of a genuine Darwinian explanation based on observed variation and selection, what we are in fact typically given is a low-grade organicist theory in which it is vaguely assumed that adaptive traits will automatically emerge by some compulsion from the environment or because societies are like organisms and therefore are automatically well-co-ordinated. Nor is any attention given to the extent of competition between societies, or to the penalties of failure and to how, exactly, maladaptive institutions will be weeded out. Again, it is simply assumed that they will disappear.

We must therefore challenge the basic assumption that competition for survival between different ways of doing and thinking in human society has always been very severe, weeding out the maladaptive and selecting the fittest, whereas we often have *the survival of the mediocre*. In our modern capitalist world of rapid innovation, financial rewards for commercial success, and advanced communication there is obviously a very high level of competition; this is true not only of goods and services, but of the market place of ideas and our notions of how we should live. These conditions, however, are highly unusual. In earlier periods, and especially in small, technologically primitive societies, the rate of innovation is very slow with few alternatives to choose from, and, just as important, a number of different ways of doing things may all be viable, so that the competition between them is actually very weak. The level of competition itself, then, can vary greatly, but if this is so, then widespread customs or institutions, such as magic or the vendetta, may not necessarily have proved themselves in the rigorous struggle for survival—it may be that there are simply frequently recurring features of human nature and society that produce them. Indeed, throughout this discussion of adaptation, we have been looking at the forces of *production*, not selection, because causal explanations are always more powerful than adaptive ones.

Again, anthropologists are well aware that primitive warfare is not about conquest, so they have struggled to find all sorts of subtle ways in which primitive warfare is really adaptive, because they have believed that if something is common it *must* be adaptive. I suggest, however, that they have been trying to solve a non-problem. Primitive warfare is widespread simply because there are a number of common factors that lead to it: the ease with which people learn to hate other groups, the aggressive propensities of young males and the need of warriors and their leaders to prove themselves, lack of effective social control in acephalous societies, the self-maintaining properties of revenge-cycles, and mystical associations between vitality and the killing of enemies. Primitive warfare could continue indefinitely in many areas precisely because it was inconclusive and insufficiently lethal. A number of similar local groups, very inefficient by more advanced standards of political and military organisation, could stagger along for century after century, not really being able to do each other much harm, in a state of minimal social change. Warfare of the primitive type continues to exist indefinitely because of these factors, until the development of the state or colonial conquest replaces these forms of warfare by those of the conquest warfare that is typical of centralised governments with professional armies.

The survival of particular customs or institutions does not, then, prove that they must be better adapted, more useful, than their alternatives. They may be useless but harmless, or positively harmful but combined with other customs that *are* useful, or not so harmful that they destroy the society in question. The conviction that everything that has survived *must* be well adapted, and if only we were clever enough we would see how, often creates a credulous attitude of mind that is the reverse of scientific. Because anthropologists have been convinced that if a custom or institution survives it must, somehow, be adaptive, they have looked for any sort of beneficial effect it can have for the group. When they have found one, which is not normally very difficult, they then claim that this explains its existence, regardless of the people's own explanations which are regarded as superficial and unscientific. Anthropology is littered with feeble explanations of vengeance, warfare, cannibalism, ceremonial exchange, religion, divination, sacred cows and so on, based on their assumed survival value, and which entirely ignore their actual historical origins and the beliefs of the people themselves.

For example, beliefs in witchcraft, magic, divination, evil spirits, the ghosts of ancestors, gods, and so on are obviously very common in primitive society. For modern Westerners, of course, this is all superstitious nonsense, but if they are just illusions why, then, have such beliefs been more or less universal until modern times? The standard answer has been that they were selected for because, despite being illusions, they had useful results in reinforcing social solidarity (as when people perform rituals together, or believe that supernatural beings punish wrongdoers), or, as in the case of divination and magic, give people confidence when faced with a threatening environment.

There was never any attempt to produce serious, systematic evidence in support of this theory of selection: no one could give examples of tribes morally disintegrating because they did not believe in supernatural punishments, or villages paralysed with fear because they had abandoned magic. It was simply assumed that every form of belief must be adaptive because, if it were not, then it would have been eliminated by natural selection. The basic weakness of the selectionist theory (besides lack of evidence), is that the comfort-value of beliefs, or their contribution to social solidarity, *can't explain why people should actually find them credible in the first place.* People may gain confidence from burning an enemy's hair-clippings, but why do people in so many societies think that this sort of procedure will actually harm the victim? No doubt a Tauade, walking along a path, who recites a spell to reach his destination more quickly (without walking faster) does so because it makes him feel more buoyant and optimistic, but this does not explain why he thinks that words in themselves have power over events, and why he does not understand the relation between time, speed, and distance.

It is *these assumptions about reality that are fundamental*, and we can only hope to explain them by looking more closely at how our understanding of the world develops, not by speculating on the adaptive value of optimism and general self-confidence in the struggle for survival. The obvious conclusion is that these, and other primitive beliefs, are universal, not because they provide some selective advantage, but simply because human beings find it very easy to think in this way, as we shall see later when we examine primitive thought in more detail in Chapter IV.

The broad conclusion of this section, moreover, is that since adaptation fails to explain cultural traits unless they are the results of conscious choice, then explanations that invoke natural selection can also have no basis in fact.

7. Inheritance, social and biological

The Darwinian emphasis on the retention of adaptive traits by successive generations means that "The linchpin that holds the selectionist paradigm together is the reduction of society and culture to systems of inheritance" (Fracchia & Lewontin 2005:18). The Selectionists define what is "inherited" as instructions or information, and the major paths of transmission are basically from parents and peers, with mutations in the copying process:

Thus we have in cultural transmission the analogs to reproduction and mutation in biological entities. Ideas, languages, values, be-

*havior, and technologies, when transmitted, undergo "reproduction",
and when there is a difference between the subsequently transmitted
version of the original entity, and the original entity itself, "mutation"
has occurred (Cavalli-Sforza and Feldman 1981:10).*

In a very general sense of course it can be said that one generation
"inherits" the culture and institutions of previous generations, as the
British have inherited their political system, or English grammar. But
as an anthropologist I have to say that the remarkably abstract and
impoverished conception of cultural transmission described by Cavalli-
Sforza and Feldman (and by Richerson and Boyd) is based on the
narrow model of biological inheritance and displays very little sense
of social reality. Think for example of a child born to a prosperous
English farming family in 1900 and compare its situation to a child
born into a poor family in modern Iraq. The influence of these environments on the children will go far beyond any "instructions" or
"information", from their parents or otherwise, and encompass their
experience of a whole way of life. Furthermore, the Selectionist model
treats the individual who "inherits" his or her culture as essentially
passive to the process of enculturation, and any differences that occur
in the process of transmission as comparable to blind mutations. But
growing up is not just an accumulation of cultural mutations. As we
grow up, our active interactions with our parents are fairly rapidly
overtaken not only by those with peers and our participation in all
the social activities around us, our neighbourhood and its various
people, the schools we attend, literacy, the technology, our economic
circumstances, and the whole range of life. In what convincing way,
for example, can the experience of events such as World War II, or the
development and experience of the computer and the Internet, or the
expansion of the social media be incorporated into the "inheritance"
model of social continuity?

We may, for example, be taught as teen-agers about the liberal
notion of "the market-place of ideas", of rational debate as the way

that civilised people settle their differences of opinion and reach a more adequate understanding of the truth. But as we grow older and actually *experience* argument and differences of opinion we soon realise that life is much more complicated, so that some may come to the view in middle age that one opinion is as good as another, others may conclude that people are basically irrational and it is a waste of time to argue with them, while others may conclude that they themselves are basically right about everything that matters and that it is their duty to force their views upon other people for their own good. A society, in other words, is an enormously complex process in which we are involved from birth to death. It does involve the transmission of information from previous generations, but it is also a kind of giant mincing machine in which the information from our elders and previous generations are completely transformed:

> *The selectionist paradigm requires the reduction of society and culture to inheritance systems that consist of randomly varying, individual units, some of which are selected, and some not; and with society and culture thus reduced to inheritance systems, history can be reduced to "evolution". But these reductions, which are required by the selectionist paradigm, exclude much that is essential to a satisfactory historical explanation—particularly the systemic properties of society and culture and the combination of systemic logic and contingency (Fracchia & Lewontin 2005:14).*

8. Ontogeny and phylogeny

The distinction between the genes of an organism, its genotype, and its physical form, the phenotype, is fundamental in biology, because there can be no feedback between phenotype and genotype by which the organism can significantly change its genes and therefore its design in the course of a lifetime as a response to its experiences. So as a result organisms have two distinct developmental processes. The first, ontogeny, is the process of maturation by which an organism develops from fertilised egg to mature adult. The second, phylogeny, is the entirely different process by which, over many generations, the design of a species changes by evolution as the result of natural selection.

But since a society is a continuous stream of *processes*, and therefore of *events* in which individuals and their culture are inextricably linked, this has profound evolutionary consequences. Evolutionary changes in societies are produced by *the same sorts of processes* as make up the transactions of ordinary daily life, so the same individuals in the course of a single lifetime can participate in one form of political order— a monarchy, for example—and then participate in its revolutionary transition into a republic, like a reptile becoming a bird in the lifespan of a single organism. *It is as though the activities of the organism were constantly changing its genotype*: as Julian Huxley put it, a society "…is at one and the same time both soma and germ-plasm, both a mechanism of maintenance and a mechanism of reproduction or transmission" (Huxley 1956:9). So in human society there can be no distinction between self-maintenance and reproduction, or between ontogeny and phylogeny.

We might however stretch a point and say that in so far as the genes of the organism, the genotype, are responsible for its design, it would not be entirely unreasonable to say that the organisational principles of a society *function* in a roughly analogous way to the genotype, even though there is no social equivalent to the gene. If we treat, for example, the grammar of a language as a kind of linguistic genotype, it is certainly transmitted to the individual members of the culture in their daily lives, and regulates many aspects of their speech patterns but, and here is the essential difference from the genotype, in the course of those lives the interactions between individuals may also produce changes in the grammar over time, as occurred for example in the drastic simplification of Anglo-Saxon grammar after the Norman Conquest. The same is of course true of all cultural patterns, organisational principles, and so on.

9. Conclusions

When I was an Oxford undergraduate our Scientific Society invited the President of the Flat Earth Society to come and speak to us, not to taunt him but because we believed that science should listen to all points of view however eccentric. It is very much in this spirit that I have been examining what Darwinian theory has to say about cultural evolution. But just as the earth really is round and not flat, there really is a massive difference between human culture, on the one hand, and plants and animals on the other, which Selectionists try to rationalise away. They do this partly by a string of misleading metaphors: that memes are social equivalents of the gene, that genes and memes are active self-replicators, whereas bodies and minds are merely their passive vehicles, that culture is a pool of memes competing with one another for existence, and that human selection can be treated as if it were natural selection. Selectionists also make three spectacularly bad assumptions, the first being to treat variations as essentially blind and receiving no input from the rest of the culture, which means that their origins become trivial or inexplicable, whereas the sources of variations are central to the whole evolutionary process. Secondly, the idea of blind variations places the whole burden of explanation on adaptation, an extremely slippery and evasive notion, instead of where it should be, which is on causal explanations. And thirdly, the idea that cultural evolution can be summed up as populational changes in the relative frequency of traits or memes is trivial and uninteresting: no one denies that the relative frequency of traits changes in the course of evolution, but this is a conceptually impoverished theory that has nothing to tell us about the structural transformations which are at the heart of the evolutionary process, and their causes. "They attempt to mimic, for no reason beyond the desire to appear scientific, a theory from another domain, a theory whose structure is anchored in the concrete particularities of the phenomena that gave rise to it" (Fracchia and Lewontin 1999:78).

Clearly, then, Selectionism rests on a world-view that is about a good deal more than reason and evidence: a profound conviction that everything in the universe can be explained by a few ultimate principles such as Universal Darwinism. We shall return to this in more detail later at the end of Chapter III.

Notes

1. Works such as G. Basalla *The Evolution of Technology*, 1988; C. Lumsden & E. O. Wilson *Genes, Mind, and Culture: the co-evolutionary process*, 1981; R. Boyd & P. J. Richerson *Culture and the Evolutionary Process*, 1985; *Not by Genes Alone: How culture transformed human evolution*, 2006; L. L. Cavalli-Sforza & M. W. Feldman *Cultural Transmission and Evolution. A quantitative approach*, 1981; D. Dennett *Darwin's Dangerous Idea*, 1996; U. J. Jensen & R. Harré (eds.) *The Philosophy of Evolution*, 1981; P. Munz *Philosophical Darwinism. On the origin of knowledge by means of natural selection*, 1993; A. T. Rambo & K. Gillogly (eds.) *Profiles in Cultural Evolution*, 1991; R. Rindos *The Origins of Agriculture. An evolutionary perspective*, 1984; W. G. Runciman *A Treatise on Social Theory* (II), 1989, *The Social Animal*, 1998, *The Theory of Cultural and Social Selection*, 2009; S. K. Sanderson *The Evolution of Human Sociality. A Darwinian conflict perspective*, 2001; Susan Blakemore's *The Meme Machine* (1999); E. A. Smith & B. Winterhalder (eds.) *Evolutionary Ecology and Human Behavior*, 1992; Mesoudi, Whiten, & Laland, "Perspective: Is human cultural evolution Darwinian? Evidence reviewed from the perspective of *The Origin of Species*", 2004.

2. The "Central Dogma" of *molecular* biology is in fact that DNA makes RNA and RNA makes protein and never the reverse. This is not the same as the Weismann barrier, which was referring to *cellular-level* inheritance, and which involves much more than the

genes. So at the cellular level "The Weismann barrier is permeable, and organisms are capable of transmitting non-DNA inheritance" (Noble 2018:246).

3. Elsewhere (1999:xvi) he says, "The real unit of natural selection was any kind of *replicator*, any unit of which copies are made…"

Chapter II

A constructivist theory of cultural evolution

The attempt to force cultural evolution into the Darwinian strait-jacket inevitably creates a whole series of intractable problems, conceptual junk like the elusive meme, random variation, and the populational model of culture. In particular, it creates the illusion that cultural variants can compete directly with one another, whereas the actual competition takes place within human minds as they choose between alternative variants. So we have to discard the Darwinian view that deconstructs cultures into populations of bits and pieces competing with one another and replace it with a constructivist theory which concentrates on how different elements of culture are *combined* to produce higher levels of complexity. Rather than variation and natural selection we shall be looking, therefore, at self-organisation and human selection. This is an emphatically organic model of cultural evolution, and totally opposed to the populational model of the neo-Darwinists. What human selection is should be sufficiently obvious because it is going on around us all the time in every aspect of life, but we know that when a number of people are interacting, novel processes may result that have not been selected by anyone, like the behaviour of the economy in our own society. This self-organisation or complexity is an essential aspect of cultural evolution, and what it basically means is that when a number of entities (individuals or groups) are interacting according to local rules or constraints, these apparently simple systems can easily produce more complex and unsuspected forms of order or

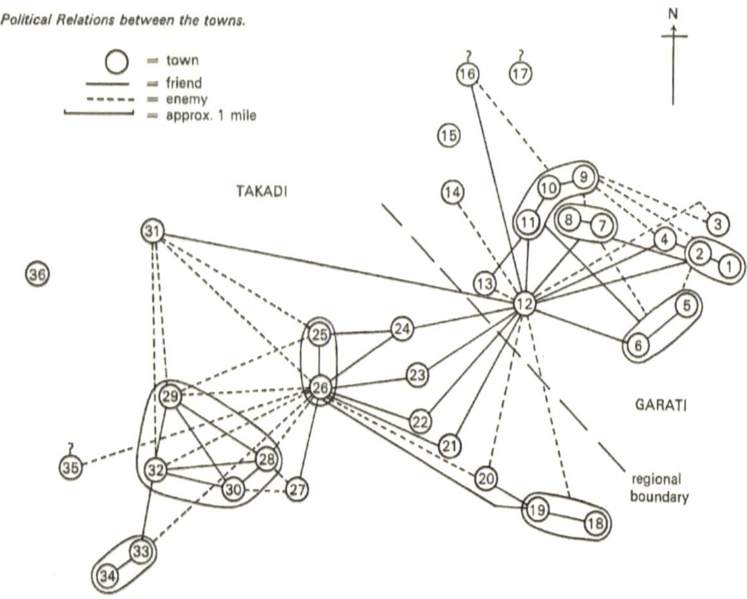

Figure 1: *Political relations between the towns.*

behaviour. Feedback loops are especially common, and it is also possible for self-organised systems to go in a dysfunctional direction (at least from the human perspective), and for this to happen abruptly. The best way of explaining what self-organisation involves in the context of human culture is by an example.

1. How human selection and self-organisation can combine

This is taken from my fieldwork among the Konso of Ethiopia (Hallpike 1970), showing how people make choices but that, nevertheless, spontaneous forms of order can emerge from a system of relations without any central direction. Fig. 1 is a map of Konso towns (some with a population of 2–3000) which, before their conquest by the Ethiopian Empire at the end of the 19th century, were politically autonomous. They were protected by massive stone walls and frequently involved in battles with one another in which the combatants had allies.

It is important to understand certain special features of this warfare. In the first place, it did not involve sieges, large massacres, the conquest of one town by another, or the seizure of the loser's land, so winning or losing any battle did not affect the probability of winning or losing a subsequent battle. The aim of a battle was simply for the town's warriors to gain prestige by killing a few men of the opposing town, and there was no attempt by any town to extend its sphere of political influence by the formation of large-scale leagues. Battles seem usually to have been precipitated by relatively minor provocations, such as failing to ask permission to use another town's hunting territory, or men of one town ill-treating the animals of a neighbouring town which had strayed on to their fields. Battles were typically brought to a conclusion by the intervention of ritual peace-makers.

In the map, dotted lines signify enmity and solid lines signify friendship. The map is incomplete, since while I resided in towns 2, 9, 12, and 26 I could not obtain details of alliances from some of the other towns, but it nevertheless contains sufficient data for our purposes. My informants were perfectly clear about which other towns were their allies or enemies, and the whole idea of alliances was obviously well established in their culture. It will be noted that a few allies have been ringed and this denotes that they are what I term "nuclear" alliances, that is, they have *all friends* and *all enemies* in common. They are thus internally stable, or in the terminology of graph theory, "structurally balanced". But an alliance of the form

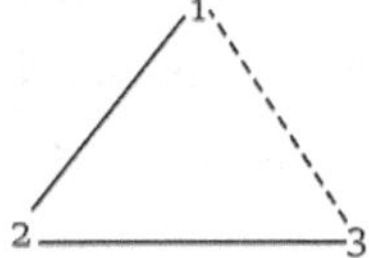

is not structurally balanced because if towns 1 and 3 were to fight each other 2 would have to choose whether to support 1 or 3, and so it could no longer remain in alliance with the one against whom it had fought. If 2 refused to fight at all it might be rejected as an ally or rated lower by 1 and 3. It will be seen that most Konso alliances are of the unbalanced form. No such conflicts, however, can arise between towns in balanced alliances which are therefore inherently stable. It will also be seen that some nuclear alliances have more members than others, and that alliances of 2 towns are the commonest:

4 members	1
2 members	6

The problem is therefore to explain why 2-member alliances should in fact be so much commoner than larger alliances. One Konso explanation of nuclear alliances was that a large town drew others into alliance with it, but if this were so one would expect the majority of nuclear alliances to have more than 2 members, especially since this would seem militarily advantageous. There are also many cases where large towns have *not* drawn their immediate neighbours into nuclear alliances.

I performed a simulation in an attempt to explain the predominance of 2-member nuclear alliances (fully described in Hallpike 1970, and see the discussion of it in Hage and Harary 1983:61–4). It began by constructing a model network of 14 towns, Fig. 2 (where superscript numbers indicate the number of a town's relations).

It was designed so that there could be a varying number of relations between towns, from 4 to 11. Towns could rate one another from 1 (very friendly) to 5 (very hostile) through 3, neutrality; ratings were then distributed at random, except that initially 1s and 5s were excluded. The simulation consisted of arranging battles between pairs of towns chosen at random and forcing a potential ally to choose between them. Town A chooses between towns B and C as an ally on the basis of its relative evaluation of each. (A town rated below 3 could not be called upon as an ally.) If the evaluation is equal, then A chooses of the basis of B's and C's evaluation of A. If both sets of evaluations are equal, A remains neutral. After the battle, the participants then revise

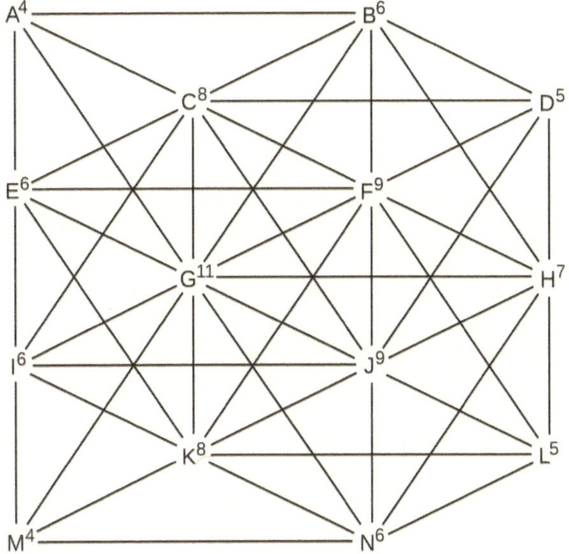

Figure 2: *Number of relations between towns.*

their evaluations of each other: the principal combatants each decrease
their mutual ratings by 1, as do allies on opposite sides, whereas allies
on the same side increased their ratings by 1. No battles were assumed
to take place between those who rated each other as 1.

Given these rules (of which a full account is given in Hallpike op.
cit., 262–7), and the arrangement of the network, the nature of the
outcome is not apparent to observation or common sense. A number of conclusions might seem possible—a state of undifferentiated
enmity or friendship, or more probably a chaotic mix of unbalanced
relationships, and also perhaps no stable patterns of alliances at the
conclusion at all but simply a permanent state of flux. It is also clear
that no single town could possibly be in control of the total system.
The 14 towns form a structure, not just a population; the relations
between them cannot be meaningfully described as those of variation
and selection; the changes that take place in them are simply a series of
responses, not adaptations, and the whole process is a product both of

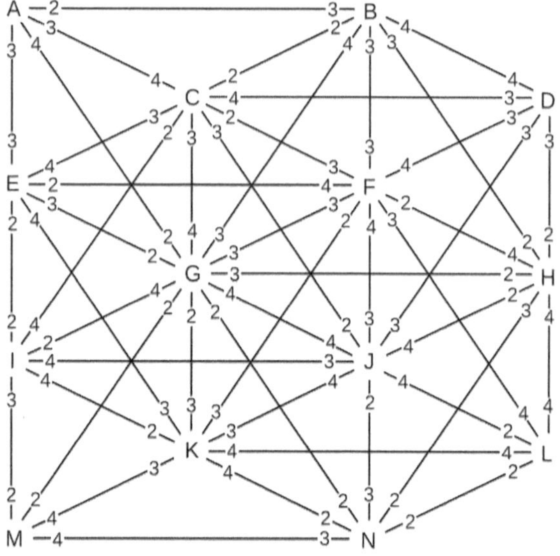

Figure 3: *Game 3: initial allocations of rankings*

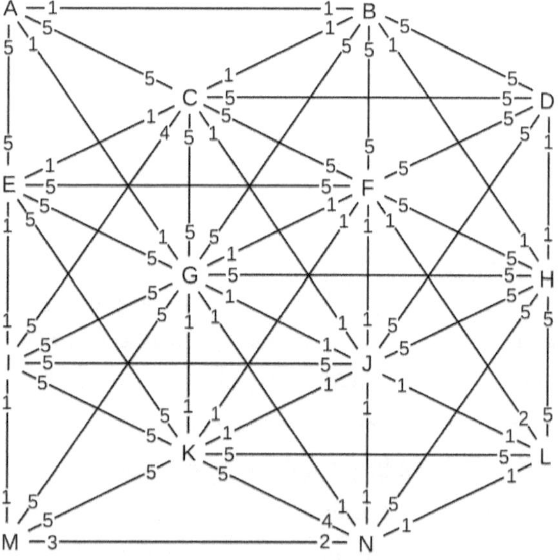

Figure 4: *Game 3: final distributions of rankings*

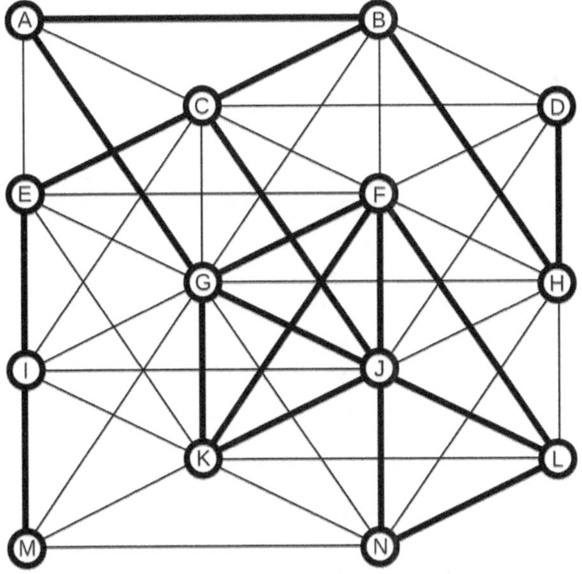

Figure 5: *All alliances (shown by thick lines)*

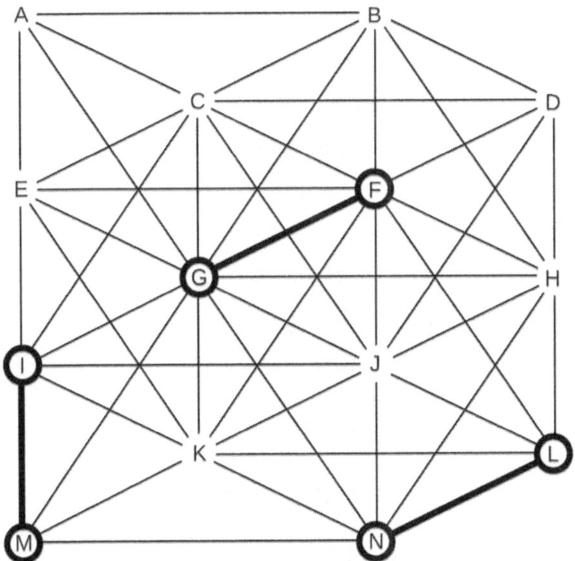

Figure 6: *Nuclear alliances*

conscious choice and self-organisation in which *people can choose but their choices are also radically constrained by their social relationships and their cultural norms.*

The simulation or "game" was in fact played 3 times, with different sets of random numbers on each occasion, but in each case a final state of equilibrium was reached quite quickly with almost all relations either 5 or 1, with a number of unbalanced relationships and a small number of nuclear alliances as well. For example, game 3 ended as shown in Figures 4–6.

If we compare the initial distribution of rankings with the final distribution we shall see that their relative frequencies change drastically:

Initial		Final	
1	0	1	39
2	31	2	2
3	33	3	1
4	30	4	2
5	0	5	50

This is what Darwinists such as Richerson and Boyd think is the essence of evolutionary change but all it tells us is that there has been a marked polarisation of relations without explaining how this has occurred. What is of real social importance is that the system always comes into a final equilibrium, and that, as in the Konso situation, there is a marked preponderance of 2-member nuclear alliances over 3-member alliances (9:3) in the 3 games:

4 member	0%
3 member	25%
2 member	75%

(In one of the games an isolated town also appeared, as is the case with town 31 in the map, whose alliance with 12 had no military significance.)[1]

The reason for the preponderance of 2-member alliances turns out to be fairly straightforward: it has nothing to do with selection but is simply because 2-member alliances have fewer of those contradictions in their alliances that create structural imbalance than do alliances with 3 or 4 members, so that it is easier for 2-member alliances to form.

The use of random number tables in this simulation acknowledges that chance is a constant factor in social life, but the essentially similar conclusions of each of the games shows that the system operates in a consistent way regardless of the random element. Each town can be said to have free will, but each town is also interacting with all its neighbours and this system of interactions has its own properties which produce consistent results. 2-member alliances are therefore not more numerous than 3-member ones because they are better adapted or "fitter" but simply because they emerge more easily from the system. This little study is therefore a good example of what I mean by the combination of human selection and self-organisation, in which new but unplanned formations can be generated, and it can be observed again less formally in the way the Konso residence pattern shifted from scattered homesteads to the walled towns of the present day.

Archaeological remains show that before the towns existed the residence pattern was of scattered family homesteads (Hallpike 2008a:81). The towns developed at the end of the 16th century when attacks on horseback by the Oromo peoples generated a defensive nucleation in one area, Buso, which built protective walls to resist the horses. The threat from these invaders seems to have faded after a few years, but the warrior culture of the Konso led the neighbours of Buso to imitate it and build their own walls, and this was repeated across the Konso territory. As in any arms race, no one can afford to be left behind, but it is distinctly possible that this nucleation into towns actually increased organised conflict, which then generated the system of town alliances that we have examined.

Before the towns emerged it seems that the Konso lived in kin groups quite close to their *poqalla*, or lineage head, and that there were a number of such kin-groups in the same neighbourhood. Members of the East Cushitic language family, such as the Konso, are notable for placing great emphasis on the importance of neighbourhood ties, as well as those of kinship, and it seems that these kin groups performed ritual services for each other, particularly burying each other's dead. There was also an age-grading system in operation which would have further united these neighbours in the shared functions of warriors and elders. So the pre-existing social organisation and culture made it quite easy for these neighbours to come together more closely in large protective aggregations, while the extremely stony nature of the terrain made it very easy to construct defensive walls, which used the same techniques as they had traditionally employed in building the elaborate stone terraces for their fields.

Now that we have seen an example of self-organisation and human selection in action we can look more broadly at the kinds of structural transformation that are involved in cultural evolution, and the basic principle of emergent but unplanned order will be shown to operate more generally in cultural evolution.

Many readers will recognise that the whole idea of self-organisation is in the tradition of general systems theory, and what has come to be known as "Complexity"[2]. In understanding such systems the notion of an environment is not central, in the way that it is in natural selection, and in many ways it can be said that the entities within the system are each other's environment which is therefore constantly shifting and may even be transformed. The entities of a system are more than a population because they are interacting with one another, and while some features of a system may become commoner than others this is not because they can be said to have been selected, in any meaningful way, but *produced*. And what is significant in self-organised systems is not necessarily how common something is but *what it leads to or facilitates*, and while there may be an important random or accidental element in the system this is quite compatible with deterministic outcomes.

2. A constructivist theory of cultural evolution

Societies and cultures are not, then, "populations" of traits in the Darwinian sense but have a structure, and cultural evolution is not about the selection of traits but very much a matter of how they combine in *the transformation of structures*, from simple cases like the changing residence pattern of the Konso, to major processes like the emergence of the state from a tribal society, or a monetary economy from a pre-monetary society. A constructivist theory builds on all those distinctive features of human culture listed in the previous chapter, and begins by recognising that societies have far lower standards of efficiency than organisms and far greater tolerance of dysfunction, and therefore assumes that a number of variants may all be capable of survival, especially in pre-state societies. In tribal society especially, where technology is so simple and communities are small, there is great latitude for many organisational variations, all of which will work after a fashion, because social groups can be organised around certain simple principles of order based on descent, relative age, birth order, and gender.

I call this *the survival of the mediocre*, and it liberates us from the Darwinian obsession with adaptation. While emphasis on the importance of the mediocre is absurd in the context of neo-Darwinian orthodoxy, it is of great importance in the very different theory that I am advancing because it allows the survival of traits of no particular value for a time, but which nevertheless have great *evolutionary potential*, when conditions have changed, that would be lost if they were prematurely weeded out. The significant issue, then, is not so much the *survival* of an innovation, but what developments it can make possible, what significant effects it has on the rest of the society while it is around, and what it can subsequently lead to, either in itself or in combination with other traits, like the steam engine which has passed into history but which made the Industrial Revolution possible. The great significance of agriculture, clans, cities, states, steam engines and electricity, for example, lay in what further developments they made possible, not just in how successful they were themselves. By contrast, slavery was also very common in the ancient world, but in evolutionary terms led nowhere.

But we also have to ask how these various traits originated in the first place. Here we should note that *doing what is easiest*, physically, socially, and cognitively, is a basic principle of a constructive model of social evolution and quite the opposite of random or blind innovation (and is also very compatible with the idea of a genetically-based human nature). Again, instead of the Darwinian model of cultural innovation as the gradual accumulation of small random variations like organic adaptations, our model assumes individual inventiveness and *the novel combination of existing cultural traits*, or those borrowed from other cultures. This is why it is a good thing that a number of variants can survive to be available for novel combinations and for *the accumulation of necessary conditions*. This does not mean necessary for survival but for further development, and is a very general principle of cultural evolution, as different as possible from the picture of cultural evolution as merely changes in the relative frequency of traits.

In many cases something discovered or invented for a particular purpose may also may have important applications that were never thought of by the original innovators, that is, it will have *multiple possible uses* not just the one for which it was first used—control of fire being an obvious example. Initially used to cook food, very much later it also laid the foundations for agriculture, not only by burning the forest and preparing the ground, but because the plants that were most suitable for cultivation by the first farmers—cereals, tubers, and pulses—were also those with a high starch content that were therefore essentially inedible unless they were first cooked. So, no fire, no agriculture and, for that matter, no pottery, metals, glass or ultimately steam power.

At this point the question may well be asked, "If in primitive society more or less anything goes, why should social evolution lead in any direction at all?" and since every society is unique how can there have been a single evolutionary pathway to the literate civilisations of the ancient world, for example. One important basis for direction is that the major innovations in social evolution such as agriculture, lineal descent groups, urbanisation, conquest warfare, the state, a literate elite, and monumental architecture all have a number of different properties, and this means that they have various opportunities to develop from different origins, and by different routes. This is known as *equifinality*[3], a familiar concept in systems theory, where the final state can be reached from different starting points and by a variety of pathways. But, having developed, they nevertheless all have the *same* evolutionary potential for producing greater political centralisation and all the other aspects of social organisation and culture that are typical of the state, regardless of their particular local histories.

The evolutionary pathway followed by each society is, however, to some extent determined by how it starts out, by the historical peculiarities of its early stages which may stamp themselves on its subsequent development. Some specific features of a particular society's organisation or belief system, *core principles*, can therefore make it easy or difficult for it to develop hereditary political leadership, or the state, or science, or capitalism. Cultural evolution is certainly not some unitary, general process that is going to be the same everywhere, regardless of local circumstances.

The constructivist theory of cultural evolution I am putting forward is also an example of a non-linear causal system, as distinct from a linear one. An example of linear causality is a row of dominoes where the first one in pushed over and knocks down all the others in succession, but the process only goes in one direction and can't be reversed. In the same way, a mutation in a gene produces a change in the organism, but there is no feedback, no possibility of the organism or the environment in turn producing any changes in the gene. So causality can only go in one direction $A \rightarrow B \rightarrow C$, which is extremely easy to understand and so has a particular appeal to those with a craving for simplicity.

However, in the discussion of selectionism in the previous chapter I argued that societies and cultures are not like this at all because they are essentially what are called *non-linear* systems. In these, effects can also react on causes, or go in more than one direction, $A \leftrightarrow B \leftrightarrow C \leftrightarrow A$ etc. so that equifinality and feedback are also typical features of non-linear systems.

It is for this reason that I have avoided all the classic "prime mover" theories of cultural evolution—population growth, geography and environmental determinism, energy-harnessing, technology, warfare, and class conflict. While these factors *in combination* have been of great importance in the total process, it has been shown time and again that taken in isolation they are quite inadequate to explain it because they all rely on linear causal models.

3. Structural transformations

The development of complex literate civilisation depends, in particular, on very large increases in the size of populations and changes in the mode of subsistence to make this possible, and also, therefore, on the means of controlling and co-ordinating these greatly increased numbers. This depends in turn on the formation of corporate groups and on the centralisation of political authority, ultimately in the form of the state, in order to provide a stable social organisation in which all the other characteristics of civilisation can flourish. To see how this happens we can now look in more detail at the transformations of social structure that often occurred in the earlier stages of social evolution, with particular attention to this development of political authority and the associated development of corporate groups because these form the underlying structure that holds it all together.

On a global scale, the adoption of agriculture and the domestication of animals laid the foundations for much larger and more permanently settled groups than could be supported by hunting and gathering. New property relations with the land under agriculture made possible the development of corporate groups such as clans and lineages, which were the basis of hereditary authority, and these and other conditions, such the development of an economic surplus through tribute, conquest warfare, a much greater division of labour, and trade, in turn laid the foundations for the emergence of the state. Because the state could control large populations, and extract a correspondingly large economic surplus from them, this in turn created a new set of conditions, including urbanisation and in some cases writing, that could form the basis of literate civilisation and high culture, including the development of philosophy and the world religions. This process resulted in fairly similar developments independently in different parts of the world. In a highly simplified form we can summarise the basic social transformations culminating in the early state as:

I. Atomistic societies

These mainly comprise hunter-gatherer bands, but are also found in some simple farming societies, especially in Papua New Guinea.

1. People place their main emphasis on their own individual interests and relationships, and on freedom from, or avoidance of, social constraint.
2. Interpersonal relations are marked by reserve and caution, and often by strain and envy.
3. Group structures are very weak beyond the range of immediate kin. When attempts at larger scale organisation are made, they often fail because people are unready or unwilling to collaborate and co-operate, and reluctant to commit to large groups.
4. Direct exchange and reciprocity are strongly emphasised.
5. Such leadership as exists is generally weak and ineffectual, and we do not find inherited authority roles.
6. Authoritative mediation in disputes is generally lacking.
7. Classification of the natural and social worlds is unsystematic.

In these societies individual ties are paramount, and group structures are weakly articulated, and close sympathy and trust would not go much beyond the extended family. There are no judicial institutions, or persons who have the authority to act as go-between, or to mediate or arbitrate in disputes. Disputes are settled by public pressure and ridicule which may involve some discussion; mutual avoidance; payment of compensation; and vengeance, which may be formal, as when the wrong-doer permits the victim some limited physical retaliation before witnesses, or informal, involving assault or homicide.

While we may find richly developed cosmologies in these societies, and beliefs in many types of supernatural beings, these beings are not linked with groups or with social authority, as it might be with the elders or chiefs, nor are they associated in any significant way with the norms of proper conduct. While some forms of behaviour may be believed to incur the anger of supernatural beings, and therefore to incur unpleasant consequences for the offender and possibly the whole community, a list of such religious offences in any of these societies would not be significantly correlated with those types of act which are condemned from the social point view—assault, theft, quarrelsomeness, and so on—but are basically violations of taboos.

II. Societies of corporate order (tribes)

The term "corporate order" is intended to stress the emergence, associated in particular with the intensification of agriculture, of a clear organisational structure based on well-defined corporate groups and their associated leadership and dispute settlement procedures. Social organisation often takes the form of considerably larger residential communities than are found in atomistic societies, normally based on agriculture, which may be quite advanced. A variety of *corporate groups* are typically based on kinship and descent, relative age and birth-order, friendship, and gender. They are considerably wider in membership than the familistic and co-operative groups of atomistic societies, and their internal solidarity both protects and controls their individual members. People now relate to one another as members of specific groups and categories, not simply as the fairly free-floating individuals of atomistic societies.

There are typically strong norms of loyalty and co-operation with members of one's kin-group, neighbourhood, working-party and age-set, for example, with well-defined expectations of behaviour for the members of each type of group, and sanctions for defaulters. In societies based on corporate order, balanced reciprocity, especially that involving gift exchanges between individuals, often loses much of the importance which it has in atomistic societies. It tends to become transformed into formal gifts between groups for specific and limited purposes, notably for marriage payments and blood compensation, into exchanges between the heads of descent groups, into vertical exchange in the form of tribute from commoners to chiefs, or lineage members to lineage heads, and into generalised reciprocity so that there are strong norms of co-operation and friendliness which do not rest on dyadic relations between individuals. In all these cases however the basic norm of reciprocity is preserved, so that lineage heads and chiefs are seen as returning what is given them either through distribution of largesse, or by the services which they perform for society or for groups within society.

Rituals, especially related to the agricultural year, become much more important and clan heads, elders, or priests play an important part in them. Ancestors and divinities also become much more significant as enforcers of the moral order, especially against murderers, thieves, and oath-breakers. Religion becomes linked with the emergence of *authority* in the form of specific offices, which become clearly defined and, very importantly, *legitimated* by religious status, descent, seniority, or election. Clan and lineage heads, village councils, and the special roles of elders are typical examples. With increased political authority there can arise more effective judicial procedures, involving the mandatory intervention by third parties, usually village councils and heads of descent groups, who typically function not only as mediators in private disputes but also as the agents of the political group as a whole to punish those offences against the group which impair its solidarity and harmony. Debate in such tribunals allows the development of articulate norms of conduct binding on all group members, and which can be appealed to in disputes.

In both atomistic and tribal societies we find that very similar social structures simply repeat themselves across the landscape, whether they be hunter-gatherer bands, or clan-based residential groupings like Konso towns or the very small Tauade tribes. The emergence of political centralisation, however, introduces a major change in which these small homogeneous local groupings are incorporated in a broader social organisation.

III. Early states

The evolutionary importance of the state was that for the first time it allowed the accumulation of large amounts of wealth, military power, and organisational capacity to be combined under centralised control and was therefore the essential basis of advanced civilisation. The emergence of the state introduced a new social landscape in which rulers could maintain their control over their subjects, if necessary, by armed force and could also conquer neighbouring societies. The repetitious "cloning" across the landscape of small local political units of tribal societies gave place to a hierarchy of districts with the king's court at the top. But although war and conquest were fundamental duties of kings, they could not rule their people by force alone, and had to be legitimated by descent from the royal line and by religious status. Religion was of the first importance not only as a prime factor in the legitimation of political authority, but as a facilitator of social co-operation. As a cultural force, religion can be the basis of social cohesion over a much larger area than that controlled by political authority alone. So the Konso towns are grouped into regions at the head of which is a great *poqalla*, who has purely ritual authority.

A state also develops more formal and elaborate legal mechanisms because of those social control problems inherent in the expansion of the social unit to a much larger scale. Giving justice to his people is one of the normal duties of kings in early states. There is an orientation toward authority and especially law, and right behaviour consists of doing one's duty, showing respect for authority, and maintaining the given social order for its own sake.

While kings had to be supported by a nobility and some kind of priesthood, and, increasingly, by an administrative system, the possibility of one man or small group directing a society and controlling its revenues had profound implications for the human race because it laid the foundations for the central planning and elaboration of government, law, religious organisation, and warfare. For example, soldiers might need to be recruited, fed, and commanded, taxes to be collected, and records kept, land surveyed, perhaps a census taken, local administrators appointed and prevented from rebelling, communications between the royal court and the local districts maintained, large-scale public works organised and paid for, a system of law courts established, and all this required a rational administrative apparatus rather than the symbolic organisation of tribal society based on descent, seniority, age, and gender.

The state was supported by the economic surplus that was extracted compulsorily from the peasantry by taxes, rents, and compulsory labour. Its ability to create these surpluses through general exploitation of the peasants made it the essential basis for a high level of craftsmanship and literate civilisation. This eventually made possible the monumental architecture of temples and palaces, the magnificent display and expenditure of the king and the ruling classes, and stimulated the development of the arts and crafts and their associated technology. Cities developed for a number of reasons, and provided a new social environment radically different from that of rural life, where elites could co-operate and interact with one another. They were an important factor in bringing thinkers together and for the eventual rise of philosophical and religious thought, and the development of explicit and often competing ideologies about society and religion, which had never been possible in pre-literate societies.

So in time a leisured elite of nobles, priests and administrators was able to develop in some societies, and who in Egypt, Mesopotamia, China, and Central America independently discovered writing. This, ultimately, allowed the human mind to achieve its full potential in mathematics, philosophy, literature, and all the arts and sciences involved in "civilisation". To be viable, an elite of this kind had to number many hundreds, and since such people were only a minute fraction of the general population (probably less than 1%) only large societies with plenty of peasants could supply the kinds of economic surplus that were needed. Just as civilisations had to be large, they had to be based on social inequality as well: the exploitation of the masses, and the extraction of more taxes in goods or labour from them than they would have been willing to give without compulsion, was the only way in which the high cultures of the ancient world could have been built up. So we see a hierarchical class structure becoming the basic organising principle of society, while kinship and especially age institutions become subordinate to it.

The state is of such importance in cultural evolution because it is also the basic platform for true competition to emerge. Before this, primitive warfare is nothing more than an indefinite succession of skirmishes that basically leave the underlying social structures unchanged—the Tauade and the Konso being cases in point. The state provides the opportunity for the development of a much more efficient fighting force that allow it to conquer its neighbours and impose its permanent authority on them, a process that occurred all over the globe and led in many cases to the development of large empires. The cultural developments associated with this liberated religion in particular from its ties with specific social institutions and allowed it to spread to other societies, sometimes peacefully and in other cases by military conquest. So here, too, real competition emerged on the world scene, and in more recent centuries political ideologies have competed like different religions. (In all these cases, of course, it is real people who do the *actual* competing.)

The hierarchies and focal activities (see below, p.59) that are such prominent features of states also made it possible, really for the first time in history, for exceptional individuals to make their distinctive cultural mark, as radical monarchs, conquerors, inventors, thinkers, and prophets. To be sure, there have always been exceptional individuals, but until the state, and especially literate civilisation, there was only a very limited scope for them to exercise their talents.

4. The accumulation of necessary conditions

After that broad overview of basic structural transformations we can now look in more detail at some of the key factors of this process, in particular:

(a) The significance of agriculture

When an area of land is used for hunting and gathering, unless it has special resources such as fish, it can usually only support about one person per 10 square miles or more. But using land to plant crops allows people in a huge variety of locations to have settled villages and much larger groups than the 25 to 50 of foraging bands, numbering in the hundreds and thousands, and was an essential basis of urbanisation and the eventual emergence of the state. Agriculture therefore had very great evolutionary potential. Its most obvious advantage is allowing people to settle in fixed locations, and this gives us the most important clue about its origins.

People may choose to live in fixed settlements, during part or all of the year, for all sorts of reasons noted by modern anthropologists. They may initially want to live close to food-stores of nuts, acorns or grains, or to gardens of useful plants, or the location itself may be very favourable for activities such as fishing, or have other advantages that they are unwilling to give up. A whole series of craft activities, such as basket-weaving, pottery, wood-working, the making of ornaments, and more elaborate food-preparation such as pestles-and-mortars, are all more easily carried out in permanent or semi-permanent settlements. Fixed settlements are also very convenient for holding ceremonies, such as initiations or other sorts of assembly. Increasingly *permanent settlements*, then, would have had various attractions for many groups of hunter-gatherers around the world. The food surplus which can be produced by agriculture can also have other uses besides supporting permanent settlements: in systems of exchange and competitive feasting between different groups, or traded with different groups as between forest and fishing societies, or for other desired commodities such as stone for tools and shells and ochre for personal ornaments, or in the domestication of animals—the earliest agricultural sites in Highland New Guinea, for example, are associated with pigs. So there would have been many possible routes to agriculture (*equifinality*): "It is unlikely ... that the same combination of factors operated in every case, and most archaeologists today would agree that there can be no universally valid model for the adoption of agriculture" (Bray 1984:34).

Agriculture not only had enormous potential for changing people's settlement patterns and population size but also their social relationships because it enhanced co-operation through such activities as clearing forests, preparing the soil, building fences and houses, and harvesting crops. It seems to be a universal rule that mingling one's labour with something, like clearing land or planting trees, establishes a good claim to ownership of it, by a group or an individual, and the idea that these rights can be perpetuated by inheritance is also universal. We can see here a profound process of self-organisation taking place, in which individual choices are nevertheless moulded by the logic of their situation, and which led to the formation of groups based on kinship.

(b) The genesis of corporate groups

A very common form of social grouping in tribal society is by lineal descent, which means reckoning descent either through males alone ("patrilineal"), or, much more rarely, through females alone ("matrilineal"). This produces clans and sub-clans or lineages which control access to property and resources, and these kin groups easily become linked to a simple principle of seniority as well. This is because eldest brothers typically dominate younger brothers. This is neither adaptive nor maladaptive, but is just a matter of people doing what is easiest for them in the circumstances and, especially in primitive society, where there are likely to be several years between births, the eldest son will have a great natural advantage over his younger brothers, who will in turn naturally tend to defer to him. Among hunter-gatherers this embryonic form of seniority has nothing to build on, because there is no group property to inherit or control, and no formal office of leadership, but in the circumstances of agriculture we now have the possibility of senior lines developing within a clan or lineage, with some sort of political office being inherited by the eldest sons of eldest sons descending from the founding ancestor.

The founder of a descent group has special status as being first, and whose fertility is expressed in his descendants, who are like a great tree springing up from a potent root. The ghosts of the lineage founder and other ancestors are widely believed to have power to punish and reward descendants; ancestor worship is very common, and the head of the lineage or clan may therefore have ritual responsibility for blessing his kinsmen and their fields, crops, and animals, as well as settling their disputes and allocating the descent group's land. Social authority seems very easily to acquire ritual status as well, and even New Guinea Big Men, who do not formally inherit their status, still had some mystical powers and qualities. None of all this was the result of variation and natural selection but of self-organisation and human selection; the formation of descent groups around property was the easiest and immediate route for organising access to land and resources, seniority of birth is just an inevitable result of the elementary dynamics of family relations, and human beings seem naturally to ascribe ritual status to those in authority.

Descent groups can also the basis of radical inequality: for example, one clan may be considered superior to all the others because their ancestors were the original inhabitants of the group territory, and allowed the ancestors of the other clans to come and live there. Some clans may be regarded as the begetters of junior clans, or some clans may have special functions, such as priests or war-leaders, and the leader of the senior clan may become a paramount chief, owed at least ritual respect.

But there is another form of corporate group that cuts across kin groups and which is based on age or generational seniority. Imagine a group of teen-age boys (and age systems are especially concerned with boys being initiated into manhood), and their "set" being given a name. Maybe five or so years later the next group is initiated and also given its own name. In time what we have is a sequence or hierarchy of age-sets, with old men at the top and boys at the bottom. The different age sets also have different functions in the society, with the most senior sets having retired from political life, the next most senior acting as elders and councillors, taking decisions on community matters and hearing disputes; and the junior sets below them acting as the warriors.

Whereas descent groups tend to divide the community, and easily develop inequalities of status, age-systems do the opposite, uniting the different kin groups, and being essentially egalitarian. While elders of course exist in kin groups these most commonly produce chiefs of some sort, whereas in age-systems any chief would have to be elected, and political authority is typically held by councils of elders. As we shall see, age-systems are therefore an obstacle to the centralisation of political authority.

In many societies the men may form corporate groups, centred on the men's house where they may spend a good deal of time together and sleep at night, and may perform rituals from which women are excluded, or may be friendship groups of men who work together in the fields and gardens. There are always residential groups, of course, and there may also be hereditary groups of craftspeople, such as potters, smiths, and weavers.

People in these societies can therefore be members of a number of several different groups, and anthropologists have long maintained that what they call "cross-cutting ties", or competing loyalties help to maintain social order. For example, members of clan A may inter-marry with members of clan B, so that if the two clans are in danger of fighting the marriage ties can be a major factor in making peace, and the same principle certainly operates very widely to all sorts of other group membership. Clearly, it is the product of self-organisation, and could not be a deliberate strategy, and these different forms of corporate groups and their networks of relationships allowed much larger populations to be co-ordinated than was possible with band societies, and we will now see how this was achieved.

(c) The emergence of hierarchical structures and political authority

These new conditions of tribal societies also laid the foundations for a whole range of other new conditions. The members of small groups of up to 50 or so can relate to one another on an individual basis, but larger groups require more elaborate modes of organisation and social categories because individuals cannot cope mentally with the exponential increase in the number of social relationships that is generated by the increased population. The people will not be conscious of this problem, however, and the immediate focus of these various groups will be straightforward practical issues such as the control and inheritance of resources, defence, leadership, and co-operation. But these groups of primitive society have another, hidden property of which their members are also most unlikely to be aware, but which has great evolutionary potential. This is their ability to allow people to simplify the number of relationships that are generated by these much larger populations.

Here we need to understand an important mathematical property of groups of any type, human or non-human, which is that whereas group membership increases arithmetically, the number of relations between the group members increases exponentially. The actual formula is $\frac{1}{2}(n^2 - n)$, where n is the number of members in the group, so if there are, say, 4 members in a group, then $4^2 = 16$, minus 4, $= 12$, and divided by 2 $= 6$. The number of possible relationships between all members of the group will therefore be 6, as we can see in this illustration of a nuclear family:

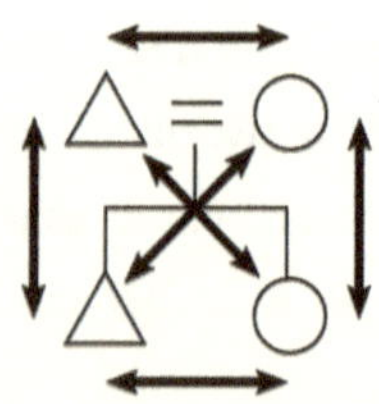

If we add one more member to the group, making it 5, the number of possible relations is not 7, but 10; and if we add 5 more members to produce a group of 10, the number of possible relations is 45, and so on, so that a group of 50 has 1225 possible relations:

n	PRs
2	1
3	3
4	6
5	10
6	15
7	21
10	45
20	190
30	435
50	1225

One of the results of this is that the number of possible relationships—alliances and disputes—increases exponentially as well, and another result is that individuals, as we have noted, start having major mental difficulties in keeping track of all the possible relationships involved. The simplest way of dealing with this problem is to lump people together in groups and categories which can be treated as single units for certain purposes, rather like a folder of documents in a filing system, so that instead of having hundreds of papers lying about we can bundle them up under a few headings. The commonest of these groups are clans and lineages, age groups, residential groups, and associations based on gender, such as men's societies. But groups where every member has to interact with every other are difficult to co-ordinate when their numbers rise much above 20: "Most of the organised groups in any society are found within the limits of the small group [of about 20]. These include practically all households, playgroups, cliques, gangs, councils, and companies. Also included are the basic units of larger economic, military, and political organisations: work crews, infantry platoons, and precinct committees" (Caplow 1957:487). So if a tribe of many hundreds or even thousands is divided into a handful of descent groups and residential groups this represents an enormous conceptual simplification, and negotiations between different groups are vastly simplified if a single spokesman can represent each group.

In the same way coordinating a number of people is much easier if there is also a hierarchical chain of information and authority. Suppose, for example, that we have a group of 8 members, and an item of information has to be communicated to them all. If there is no established sequence of individuals for this, then the total number of interactions must be 28, and in this case many people will be telling others what they already know. This can be reduced if one member has the job of passing on information to all the others, or if there is a fixed sequence:

This puts a considerable strain on one member, however, whereas in a fixed sequence this is avoided:

This is very slow, however, and an alternative arrangement is a hierarchy:

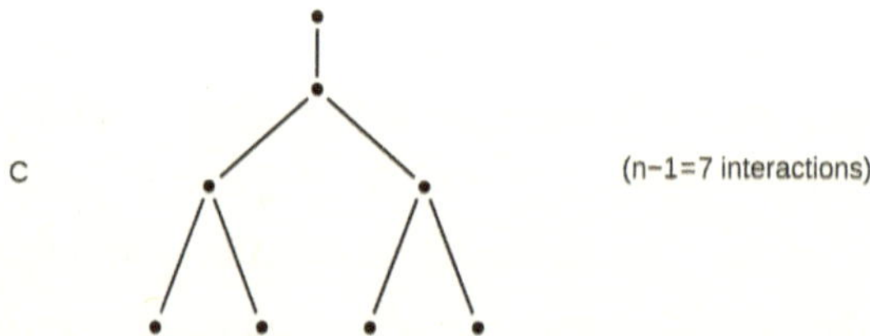

The number of interactions remains the same, but the process is greatly speeded up by the introduction of parallel chains, while the workload is only two members each.

Type A is often found in societies where a spokesman represents a group. If we have two groups of 50 members each, and if these groups want to negotiate something, such as terms of peace or compensation, then if all members (total 100) want to talk to one another the total number of possible relationships will be 4950, whereas if each group were represented by a spokesman to whom each member of the group gave his opinion, the total number of possible relations with only be 99, a 50-fold reduction. Groups of this type would count as Medium Groups, of 50–1000, whose distinctive feature is that, unlike Small Groups, all members do not interact with each other, but instead one or a few leaders may interact with all members of the group. So as groups increase in size, an asymmetry between leaders and the rest of the membership tends to develop, whereby the leader or a small group of leaders will be recognised by their followers, but the leader or leaders will not have the time to interact closely with all their followers individually.

Type C, hierarchy, is also very common, because it applies as well to groups as to individual members, and we are quite familiar with it as the way in which all large institutions are organised. Of course, the people involved will have no idea of the special properties of the social networks and hierarchies and would simply, as individuals, have had difficulty in coping with the increased number of relationships, but this factor of what we can call "cognitive overload" would nevertheless have made the development of more complex social organisation more acceptable. But the *immediate* reasons for the formation of clans and lineages were the practicalities of controlling and inheriting property, the status of the eldest son, initiation, totemic beliefs, and so on. This is just another example of how people create institutions for limited but perfectly understandable purposes and do not realise their further implications, which allow the control and coordination of the far larger populations that the agricultural way of life made possible.

Yet another condition is supplied by the fact that descent is not just social, but has very strong biological associations, and we often find that descent groups are linked with the natural world by a variety of totems. But the "nature" of primitive society is not the coldly neutral nature of modern science, but a nature permeated by supernatural forces and symbolic values, and so the leaders of descent groups are often thought to have the power to bless their kinsmen. All over the world, in Polynesia, China, Africa, and the Americas, for example, we find that political leadership is based on seniority of descent and religious status, and this in turn forms the political basis of the early state.

We can therefore see how it is possible for hereditary political leaders to develop on the basis of lineal descent groups and seniority, supported by religious status. These beliefs and values give such leaders the property of *legitimacy*, which is the idea that their authority is rightfully or properly exercised, and is an essential support for power and social inequality in all societies. Typical functions of such leaders would be presiding over the allocation of clan land, dispute settlement, spokesmanship for their group, and ritual responsibilities.

One of the most important structural features of social evolution, therefore, is the development and centralisation of power. We tend to think of power as something imposed from the top down, but this is a late development with the state. It originates, however, as a function of *dependency*, the product of situations in which individuals are not self-sufficient. In hunter-gatherer societies the scope for power is very limited indeed, because everyone has access to the necessities of life, but with the adoption of agriculture and the domestication of animals people cease to be self-sufficient in many respects. For example, novel property relations develop in which access to resources is increasingly controlled by groups based on descent and residence, and their leaders. In hunter-gatherer bands, again, fighting is very small in scale, but in the larger societies of tribes the individual becomes much more dependent on his residential and descent groups for support and security, and therefore on the leaders of these groups. Yet again, access to the benefits believed to come from supernatural sources becomes, in tribal societies, increasingly monopolised by those who inherit this function, like priests and lineage heads. But in tribal society, however, political power remains relatively uncentralised and dispersed and it is the transition to the state and the centralisation of power this involves that creates a whole new range of evolutionary opportunities for the complete reorganisation of society.

Political authority is also strengthened by the economic mobilisation of the family unit, where chiefs receive tribute in the form of food and livestock, and which they redistribute to their dependents as hospitality and to relieve poverty. In subsistence economies, the family is the basic unit of labour, and can basically produce all the food, fuel, and shelter that it needs. In this situation people naturally prefer leisure to work because there is nothing they could get by working harder, and participation in social activities is the main incentive to produce more than one needs. Communal feasts and dances, rituals involving sacrifice, displays of generosity for prestige, exchange, and tribute to clan heads or others who are seen as social benefactors are typical examples. One vital aspect of social evolution therefore involves the integration of the family into wider productive networks that can eventually be used by chiefly authority to strengthen its influence and power.

(d) Warfare

We saw that primitive warfare was widespread not because it was adaptive but simply because there were a number of common factors that led to it. The real evolutionary potential of warfare in tribal society was not that it readjusted population imbalances, or that it was a source of protein, or that it worked as a form of natural selection by eliminating unfit individuals or groups or customs, or had any other pseudo-adaptive advantages, but rather that it stimulated higher levels of co-ordination within the local group than would have been needed in a situation of peace. In the first place, fear over personal safety in a milieu of chronic warfare leads people to live closer to one another than they would otherwise do, in defensive settlements such as the Konso towns, and the usual response to an increase in warfare is an increase in settlement size and group co-operation in building stockades and other defences. The war party inevitably required the co-operation of a number of adult males of every household, and fighting was, together with ceremonial exchange, one of the basic means by which wider social bonds were forged. When freedom to migrate was restricted in densely populated areas (circumscription), unlike New Guinea, dependency on one's local group and loyalty to it would obviously be intensified. Mutual dependency of this sort meant that fighting was also the basis of politics in tribal societies where alliances and enmities with other groups were crucial issues, and so it was a powerful reason for co-operation and for some men to accept the leadership of others, not only as fight leaders, but also as spokesmen for the group in peace negotiations, which were very important.

Being a successful warrior by itself could not be a source of political authority in a kin-based society, but where chiefly authority already existed, legitimated by descent and religious authority, was a very important way of enhancing the chief's political power if it could be combined with war leadership. The willingness to accept this enhancement of chiefly power would of course increase when there was a significant external threat, and so competing chiefdoms are one of the basic scenarios which encourages the centralisation of political authority. When stable inherited political authority emerged, it was the long established traditions of warfare that could be developed into a means of conquering one's neighbours by armed force, which was a principal route into the emergence of early states. None of these *consequences* of warfare were, of course, *why* people actually fought. This they did for quite other reasons that we have already examined. They were simply the consequences that were built, as it were, into the structure of tribal society.

Warfare was intimately involved with the emergence of states from their beginning, but the warfare of states was very different from that of tribes and chiefdoms (Turney-High 1971). Primitive warfare lacked discipline, and was unable to conduct extended campaigns in hostile territory and to conquer and politically subjugate the enemy. One of the essential features of state warfare, on the other hand, was conquest because their much greater resources of manpower, food, discipline, and organisation allowed states to put far more effective armies into the field, and keep them there for extended periods of time to fight campaigns of conquest. Comparatively small professional armies could conquer many times their number of tribal opponents because of their superior discipline and organisation, and the development of large organised battles, instead of the endless raids and skirmishes by the warriors of tribal societies and chiefdoms, made it possible for single, decisive battles to change the course of history. The warfare of states therefore led to far more effective competition between societies. In a survey of 21 early states Claessen (1978) found that in the vast majority of cases the ruler's status was justified by genealogy; that he had sacred status; that he was closely associated with warfare, either as the real or nominal commander; and that trade and markets were of major significance in consolidating the power of the ruler, and these are clearly among the most important of the necessary conditions for state formation.

(e) Urbanisation and focal activities

Agriculture allowed the growing size of settlements, and cities were closely associated with early states and the development of civilisation, but first we must be clear what we mean by "city". In the first place, a city is not simply a settlement of people that has grown very big. The Konso town of Degato had around 3000 inhabitants, with a defensive wall a mile in circumference, so that it was larger than the city of Bath, for example, in Roman Britain. But Degato, like all the other Konso towns, was inhabited entirely by farmers except for a tiny minority of craftsmen, and was simply a large rural settlement. The essential features of a city are not that it must have a population of, say, 10,000, or 50,000 or even 100,000, but that it functions as *an organisational centre in some wider system*, whether this be administrative, commercial, military, religious, educational, or all of these together. We can call these "focal" activities (Trigger 1972:578), and it is through them that cities become large and socially stratified, and increasingly distinct from the rural life around them. Here again I am focusing on yet another aspect of self-organisation.

The nature of farming spreads it out across the landscape because that is where crops are grown and animals reared, but focal activities, unlike farming, are most conveniently and cost-effectively carried out when they are located in one place, or at least directed from a centre. (Of course, the people actually concerned need not think in terms of cost-effectiveness, but merely take the easy route of going to where other people engaged in this activity are already located.) A very obvious example of a focal activity is a market because buyers and sellers need a fixed and well-known location where they can be sure of meeting each other. Craftsmen, too, gain no special advantage from living in a dispersed manner like farmers, and are often better off by congregating together in the vicinity of markets. All hierarchical organisations are also inherently focal because, by definition, they must have a head, and he can only operate in one place at a time. The most obvious example is a state with a royal court at its apex of government, together with its administrative apparatus dealing with taxation and the control of subordinate regions. (In some early states, however, royal courts might have no fixed capitals, but move around the kingdom to maintain order and consume their tribute.) Religious centres, too, may acquire great wealth from the offerings and pilgrimages of the faithful, like pre-Islamic Mecca, and have a large priesthood and administrative structure. As civilisation advances, cities may also become centres of learning which, again, is most convenient and effective when concentrated in key locations where scholars from widely scattered locations may congregate like

Athens, the court of the Abbasids in Baghdad, or medieval Paris and Oxford. The waging of war is another focal activity because a disciplined military force is most effectively organised by having its headquarters in one place under the direct control of its commanding officer.

It follows from what I have been saying that there were many routes (*equifinality*) to the development of cities such as mercantile or manufacturing centres, temples or other forms of religious centre, royal courts, or defensive locations, and that it is mistaken to think that they could only have originated in one way, such as being storage centres for food surpluses. The Greek city-states, for example, began as the seat of the king in a fortified settlement, the Acropolis, around which grew up the *agora* (market/assembly place) and further settlement. Others, such as those like Mohenjo Daro and Harappa of the Indus Valley, were major trading centres acting as gateways between local centres of population and long distance traders. Mecca, again, was a place of pilgrimage for centuries before Muhammad, to the sacred stone known as the Ka'aba, and was also the major town on the frankincense trade route from Southern Arabia to the Mediterranean. In Mesopotamia the temple and its associated organisation was the essential focus of the city, and a similar pattern of sacred sites can also be found in Central America and Peru. On the other hand, urban centres in ancient China seem to have been basically administrative centres established on the orders of the king.

So, if we look at the list of focal activities we can see that commerce, manufacturing, government and administration, priestly, educational and military functions can not only be carried out most conveniently in one place but are also mutually reinforcing. A religious centre with its priestly schools might well be closely linked with a temple and a royal court, with a market served by long-distance trade, and a complex local organisation of craftsmen and artisans not only linked with the market but serving the court and temple. The whole complex could well be defended by walls, with a resident body of troops. The result would almost inevitably be a very large settlement that is not just a place where people have their homes but which performs a new kind of function in society: it is the nerve centre or node in a network of communications by which governmental, commercial, religious, military and other functions are co-ordinated. (We shall see in Chapter IV that this type of social organisation has important cognitive consequences.) The result is a population with a variety of occupations, and while these may be largely hereditary we now have a population where people are mainly defined by what they *do*, and in terms of social class rather than of clan or lineage. Roman Bath was smaller than the Konso village of Degato, but it was a city in the functional sense that it was a religious and commercial centre whose population had a wide variety of occupations and where the bonds between the inhabitants were not primarily those of kinship and local land ownership, but based on membership in a common municipal enterprise.

When I first went to Konso in 1965 there was simply a small administrative village, Bakaule, where the Governor had his office, and there were a couple of bars and a trade store, with a small contingent of police, and the Mission nearby. On my return in 1997 there was now a new town, Karat, of some two and a half thousand people, which was the headquarters of the administration and a number of its departments, schools, the police, the Ethiopian Church and the Mission, and a market, with a monetary economy and a large commercial population with many stores and bars. The Konso living there were basically literate and Amharic-speaking, with some secondary schooling, and Christians, and although they still had close ties with their traditional kin and their land they were now a new elite class living a truly urban life. Karat Town was fundamentally different in type from the traditional Konso towns, which were entirely inhabited by farmers, with a few craftspeople, and still to a large extent pagan—altogether a classic example of state urbanisation.

5. Core principles

It is also obvious, however, that this accumulation of necessary conditions that we have been describing will not always go on indefinitely until every society develops the state and, eventually, industrial civilisation. Most societies did *not* spontaneously develop the state, let alone modern science and industry, and this is because in most cases the necessary conditions for these developments were not present. So stagnation and equilibrium are just as likely as evolutionary advance, and here it is important to stress that the special features, or *core principles*, of particular societies may be of great importance in how they develop. The phylogenies of species and the history of particular societies both display remarkable continuities despite a multitude of local variations, conserving existing design features while adapting to change. The evolutionary pathway followed by each society is to some extent determined by how it starts out, by the historical peculiarities of its early stages which may stamp themselves on its subsequent development. Some specific features of a particular society's organisation or belief system can therefore make it easy or difficult for it to develop hereditary political leadership, or the state, or science, or capitalism. Social evolution is certainly not some unitary, general process that is going to be the same everywhere, regardless of local circumstances.

In all societies there are some key features of social organisation and values such as descent and kinship, relative age, seniority of birth, the relations between the sexes and the generations, rules of residence, authority and leadership, ritual status, and property rights, competition, the status of the individual, honour, and warfare and warriorhood on which some rules and categories are developed, and on which different emphases will be placed. We find that in every cultural tradition there emerges a distinctive world-view, a set of "core principles" about social organisation, values, and beliefs in terms of which subsequent generations continue to interpret the world despite migrations and new environments. Comparative studies show that these core principles can last not just for hundreds but for thousands of years, and will be highly relevant to the emergence of centralised political authority (see Hallpike 1986:288–371 for a discussion of the core principles of Indo-European and Chinese society, and Kirch & Green 2001 for those of Polynesia).

For example, Polynesian and Melanesian societies are based on very different core principles, which explain why political centralisation was much more developed in Polynesia than in Melanesia, although the traditional economies of both cultural groups were very similar: horticulture based on combinations of yams, taro, breadfruit, bananas, coconuts or pandanus nuts, and pigs. In Melanesia the whole ideology of lineal descent tends to be rather vague, so that the Tauade words for "kin", for example, also meant "friend", and seniority of birth is not an important social principle:

> *The characteristic western Melanesian "tribe", that is, the ethnic-cultural entity, consists of many autonomous kinship-residential groups. Amounting on the ground to a small village or cluster of hamlets, each of these is a copy of the others in organisation, each tends to be economically self-governing, and each is the equal of the others in political status. The tribal plan is one of politically unintegrated segments—segmental (Sahlins 1963:287).*

Local residential groups tend to be small, normally limited to around two or three hundred, and a few square miles in extent. If clans exist they tend to be less important than the bonds of friendship and co-residence. Leadership is exercised by Big Men, but they are not installed in a public office by inheritance—eldest sons have no special significance—or by formal election: their influence over their followers is purely personal, and depends on the leader's individual qualities: "[A] man must be prepared to demonstrate that he possesses the kinds of skills that command respect—magical powers, gardening prowess, mastery of oratorical style, perhaps bravery in war and feud" (ibid., 291). Most important, the Big Man must be able to organise his faction to produce hospitality and food, especially pigs, in the public distribution of wealth, to gain renown for generosity. This sort of leadership is inherently unstable, because it disappears as Big Men get too old, and their competition with other Big Men can make economic demands on their own followers that leads to resentment and rebellion against the Big Man.

In Polynesia, on the other hand, "Polynesian social structures are literally built upon the principle of seniority. Kin groups are traditionally organised around the relative seniority of descent lines" (Goldman 1970:15). Patrilineal descent is very clearly defined, the superiority of the eldest son is a basic social principle, and the political structure is based on a hierarchical clan structure with hereditary chiefs of varying rank:

Local groups of the order of self-governing Melanesian communities appear in Polynesia as sub-divisions of a more inclusive political body. Smaller units are integrated into larger through a system of inter-group ranking, and the network of representative chiefs of the subdi-visions amounts to a co-ordinating political structure. So instead of the Melanesian system of small, separate, and equal political blocs, the Polynesian polity is an extensive pyramid of groups capped by the family and following of a paramount chief (Sahlins 1963:287).

Unlike the small local groups of Melanesia, the politically autonomous bodies of Polynesia typically number between 2–3,000, and the 10–20,000+ of incipient states like Tonga and Hawaii, with territories varying from tens to hundreds of square miles.

Chiefs inherit their office by primogeniture, and have a variety of traditional rights and privileges: "The chiefly lineage ruled by virtue of its genealogical connections with divinity, and chiefs were succeeded by first sons, who carried 'in the blood' the attributes of leadership [*mana*]".… "His authority came from the organisation, from an organised acquiescence in his privileges and organised means of sustaining them" (ibid., 295). He commanded the labour and land of his people by right, and did not have to build it up by reciprocal gift-giving, as did the Melanesian Big Man:

The division between small internal and larger external political sectors, upon which all big-man politics hinged, was suppressed in Polynesia by the growth of an enclaving chiefdom-at-large. A chain of command subordinating lesser chiefs and groups to greater, on the basis of inherent social rank, made local blocs or personal followings (such as were independent in Melanesia) merely dependent parts of the larger Polynesian chiefdom.... While the island or the archipelago would normally be divided into several independent chiefdoms, high-order lineage connections between them, as well as kinship ties between their paramount chiefs, provided structural avenues for at least temporary expansion of political scale, for consolidation of great into even greater chiefdoms (ibid., 294).

Monarchies could therefore develop in Tonga, Fiji, and Hawaii, and incipiently among the Maori of North Island New Zealand in response to British conquest (Gorst 2001).

It was also hard for centralised political authority to develop among the Iroquois-speaking tribes of North America. They had hereditary chiefs who were the heads of matrilineal descent groups, controlled trade routes and their clan's treasury of prestige goods, were responsible for organising public ceremonial and religious rituals, and providing generous hospitality, and acted as spokesmen for their community in diplomacy with other groups. Yet they were not paramount chiefs with significant political power because of a number of other features of Iroquoian society. In the first place, the Iroquois, like many peoples of eastern North America, made a very important distinction between peace chiefs, such as the ones I have been describing, and war chiefs who, as the name implies, were responsible for the conduct of raids, and the torture and killing of prisoners and witches. This distinction "had to do with the idea that violence and maintaining order were incompatible from the cosmological point of view".[4] The peace chiefs were elected from the chiefly line by the older women of the clan, and there was a general ethos of equality: "at all levels of Iroquoian society, care was taken to avoid the appearance of coercion or of one person being given orders by another" (Trigger 1990:132). It seems that the women of the clan tried to avoid electing chiefs who might become too ambitious, and could depose them if they did. In addition, while peace chiefs may have organised rituals of increase, they had no personal monopoly of sacred powers and many other people officiated at these rituals, while shamans were also very important sources of supernatural power.

Again, the core principles of the societies that speak East Cushitic languages of Ethiopia, such as the Konso, have some distinctive features that made it very hard for them to develop chiefdoms (Lewis 1974, Hallpike 2008a).

East Cushitic societies tend to share the following characteristics:

1. Descent groups and genealogy are not the major or dominant factors in the organisation of group action. Clans are dispersed and not the owners of demarcated territories, and they are not formally ranked.

2. On the contrary, there is an important sense of the moral demands of common residence in the conduct of everyday affairs, and co-operation is based on community membership and norms of neighbourliness, regardless of descent.

3. Freedom of association is basic, and may be expressed in voluntary associations, or in change of residence.

4. Age is a very important basis of social organisation, and all these societies have a complex form of age system known as *gada*, characterised by a fundamental concern with generational seniority.

5. Formal councils of elders are the norm, with elected leadership.

6. Leaders are elected on the basis of personal achievement.

7. A number of East Cushitic societies are primarily or exclusively pastoralist in their economies, and it is very likely that this is related historically to the development of *gada* systems, though societies like the Konso have long been intensive agriculturalists (Lewis 1974), and

8. Ritual authorities were peace-makers and could not lead or take part in warfare.

The East Cushitic social model, as already noted, made it relatively easy for the large defensive settlements of the Konso to form at the end of the 16th century at the time of the Oromo attacks, because there was already an established social organisation based on the neighbourhood, and on the *gada* system in particular, rather than on clans and descent groups alone. But it was correspondingly difficult for the early state to develop in Konso society and in all East Cushitic societies because of the relative importance of the *gada* system by comparison with the clans. There is a basic conflict between the ideologies of age and descent: that of descent is inherently unequal and divisive because we all have different ancestors, of different status, whereas the principle of age is inherently egalitarian and unifying because all men start as boys and, barring accidents, all can expect to become elders, and this is why in societies with well developed age-systems the claims of descent, and therefore of hereditary authority, are always moderated.

The regional *poqalla* presided over the age-system and performed its essential rituals for all the towns of their region, blessing its members and the pair of sacred drums that in each region were symbols of peace, and had to observe a number of taboos including the requirement to live in isolation outside the towns. They were particularly rich because they inherited especially large estates, and were given tribute by the towns of their region, and also collected tax from local markets. They could intervene as ritual peace-makers in battles between the towns, and also act as judges in disputes between individuals of different towns but, on the other hand, could not take any part in warfare, either its conduct or its planning, and had no armed supporters to enforce their decisions, because, as in the case of the Iroquois, bloodshed was seen as conflicting with their sacred status as bringers of peace. They were not the leaders of any of the towns, nor were they the heads of any of the nine clans of the Konso: these clans did not own land and the members were dispersed among all the towns, so they were not effective corporate groups that could have formed a power-base. The fact that the regional *poqalla* could not be war leaders, did not have a potential power-base in any of the towns either, and were not the owners or controllers of clan lands, which were basic factors preventing them developing into chiefs with real political authority. In addition, certain legends suggest that the Konso age system was adopted, at least partly, as a means of restraining what might become the arbitrary authority of the *poqalla*, and the age-system had a strongly egalitarian ethos.

The Konso towns were the real centres of power, and the fact that their decision-makers were elected councils of elders would not in itself have prevented one or more of them developing into miniature city-states, as those of Greece and Rome demonstrate. But none of them had sufficient man-power to be able to conquer the others and be the basis of an incipient city-state. So the political fragmentation of the towns and the political impotence of the regional *poqalla* were therefore fundamental obstacles to state-formation among the Konso.

We can see this by comparing this East Cushitic form of society with that of the West Cushitic societies, which had very different core principles:

1. Rule by a sacred king.

2. The subdivision of the kingdom into districts and sub-districts, each with its chief and sub-chief. These may be hereditary or appointed, but always derive their authority ultimately from the king.

3. A number of patrilineal, exogamous clans, which are grouped into two exogamous marriage classes, one of which ranks higher than the other. These clans have heads whose office is inherited by primogeniture from the clan founder. The despised artisan "castes" are always in special clans of their own and not dispersed among the main body of clans.

4. The clans were originally localised in specific areas of land, and while there has been an historical tendency to disperse there are still strong associations in most cases between the clans and the administrative districts, so that in some cases clan heads may also be district chiefs.

5. There is no type of age-grouping system of any kind.

6. While all these peoples have cattle their economies are primarily agricultural and based on *ensete* and cereals, and none of their economies could be described as pastoralist.

7. Ritual and military leadership could be combined (From Straube 1963).

In earlier centuries these societies were organised on the basis of sacred kingship, which was integrally associated with a system of territorial clans ranked hierarchically. It was therefore very easy for this sacred kingship to develop into the social formation of the early state when historical conditions of trade and warfare made this possible.

It is therefore very significant that whereas all the East Cushitic-speaking neighbours of the Konso had age-systems, and no kings, the West Cushitic-speaking societies all had kings and no age-systems. The clans in West Cushitic society also had much greater political importance: there was a royal clan, below which were commoner clans, with some slave clans at the bottom. Not only were West Cushitic clans of ranked status, but far from being scattered like those of the Konso, their members were all located in specific territories, with local hereditary clan leaders who controlled the allocation of land. The West Cushitic king was not only the religious head of his people, but also their war leader; in some cases it was believed that the royal dynasty had been there from the beginning of time, and in others that it had achieved its position by leading the conquest of the original inhabitants. In many of the societies speaking West Cushitic languages, then, the state did develop, notably in Kaffa and Janjero, and this is because in these societies the descent principle was paramount, residence was dependent on clan membership, the chief and subordinate clan heads controlled the land, there was no form of age-system, and the chief was not only the supreme religious figure but could also combine his religious status with that of being a war leader as well.

Polynesian and West Cushitic societies share a number of features that clearly favour political centralisation: well-defined patrilineal corporate descent groups, hierarchically organised on the basis of seniority and primogeniture, and living on their clan land; the sacred status of chiefs; the combination of sacred and military authority; and the acceptance of hereditary inequality. On the other hand, in the case of the Melanesian, Iroquois, and East Cushitic societies, descent groups are vaguely defined, or lack hierarchical structure, or are dispersed, or matrilineal, and primogeniture may not be important, while the principle of descent may be in conflict with that of age, and the ethos of the society may be basically egalitarian. Authority may not be in the form of inherited office, but have to be earned by personal qualities, and either lack sacred authority; or there may be a conflict between sacred and military authority. None of these cultural characteristics is maladaptive, but they are all hindrances to the centralisation of political authority.

6. The sources of creativity and innovation

So far we have mainly focused on the evolution of social institutions, and it is now time to look at cultural evolution more broadly, particularly at how innovation occurs. In the neo-Darwinian model only mutations in the genotype can be responsible for innovation, and this assumption unavoidably leads to the belief that evolutionary development in any particular direction has to be achieved by the gradual accumulation of small variants through the selective process, not by major leaps. In the words of Richerson and Boyd, "most complex cultural adaptations were assembled by the gradual accumulation of small variations like organic adaptations. And, the evidence convinces us that this is exactly the way most cultural change occurs" (2006:49). Well the "evidence" would convince them, wouldn't it, because Richerson and Boyd are faithful Darwinists, and Darwin had taught them that major leaps, or "hopeful monsters" are impossible.

There are in fact three major differences between complex biological and complex cultural innovations which make Darwin's ideas on the subject irrelevant. The first is that organisms can have no down-time but must be permanently viable and keep on living and reproducing, so they cannot be disassembled for major innovations while they are alive. Culture and its products, on the other hand, are not alive and so mechanical devices, for example, can be taken to pieces and left indefinitely on the inventor's workbench while he makes radical alterations to them, and the same is true of theories, books, works of art, and so on. The second is that the inventor can think and therefore can anticipate at least some of the problems his innovation may encounter in the real world, whereas nature has no foresight at all. And thirdly, the inventor has to present at least a working model of his invention to the world if he wants it to be accepted, and the same is again true of works of art, books, theories of every kind, and the teachings of religious leaders and philosophers. In the case of any significant novelty, therefore, the often lengthy research and development has to come *first*, so as to produce the intended product that actually works and will be of interest to potential users, and the modifications come later. When Newcomen was working on his steam engine he would not have got very far if he had gone round to the mine-owners with a cart-load of rods and levers and cylinders and suggested that they might be able to work something out together to make a steam-engine. He had to produce a viable steam engine first, and then convince them that it could pump the water out of their mines. Afterwards, as we know, the steam engine, like all other devices, was subject to a whole range of modifications, so that the development of human inventions is the exact opposite of biological mutations. An accumulation of small variations does not lead to a major innovation: the major innovation has first to be developed until it is ready for release, then later a series of smaller variations are made to it from experience over time. A more appropriate biological analogy for complex inventions would be the assembly of the embryo within the protective shield of an egg or a womb until it is ready to emerge into the wider world on its own.

Sometimes, again, a single revolutionary insight is enough to produce a major novelty such as the clock. Medieval monasteries had water-clocks with an alarm-bell system to awaken a monk who would then toll a large bell for midnight services. In the alarm-bell mechanism there was a wheel with a row of pins set alternately around each rim. As the wheel rotated, driven by a weight, these pins would strike first one side, and then the other, of a semicircular piece of metal on the bottom of a shaft. (See North 2005:180,181 for an illustration.) The shaft, which had a cross-piece on top, would therefore oscillate, and the ends of the cross-piece would have struck a bell, or bells. But if weights were attached to each arm of the cross-piece (perhaps to make it ring louder?) this would slow down its action, so that it could be used instead as an "escapement" to control the speed at which the wheel rotated. Essentially the action of the bell-ringing mechanism was simply reversed to turn it into an escapement. "It is easy to imagine that such a crude bell-ringing device, with a falling-weight drive left to run unchecked, suggested itself as the first mechanical escapement" (ibid., 183) which was the essential element of the clock. This controlled rotation of what was now the "escape" wheel was the basis by which the rest of the gear-train of a mechanical clock could then be regulated, powered by a weight on a cord around the axle of the driving wheel[5]. Discovery of the escapement was the fundamental key and once it had been achieved developing the rest of the clock was straightforward.

Again, Ctesibius in around 270 BC was installing a movable mirror in his father's barbershop, and to keep the mirror in place he devised some counter-weights which ran inside tubes, compressing the air within them. He was a mechanical genius who later worked at the Museum in Alexandria, and this discovery led him to invent the piston and cylinder that, with the addition of valves, could be used as a pump for raising water and draining mines, one of the fundamental mechanical devices of antiquity.

So there are plenty of major innovations, or "hopeful monsters" in cultural evolution, but we also find that many inventions involve the *combination*, the bringing together, of different elements or components from separate areas of culture. What has come to be known as Chaos Theory is a good example of what Richerson and Boyd would call "a complex cultural adaptation", but it was certainly not produced by the "gradual accumulation of small variations":

> *The discovery of chaos was made by many people, too numerous to list here. It came about because of* the conjunction of three separate developments *[my emphasis]. One was a change of scientific focus, away from simple patterns such as repetitive cycles, towards more complex kinds of behaviour. The second was the computer, which made it possible to find approximate solutions to dynamical equations easily and rapidly. The third was a new mathematical viewpoint on dynamics—a geometric rather than a numerical viewpoint. The first provided motivation, the second provided technique, and the third provided understanding (Stewart 1996:130–31).*

This combinatorial account of the origin of chaos theory, which has no resemblance to a mutation, or to the accumulation of small variations, is typical of many other analyses of how some important ideas or inventions originated by *the bringing together* of disparate factors, a notable example being the Chinese invention of gunpowder.

The three ingredients of gunpowder are saltpetre (potassium nitrate, KNO_3), sulphur, and carbon, ideally in the form of charcoal. Charcoal burns easily, and sulphur has a low ignition point of 250 °C, but the essential function of saltpetre is to supply large amounts of oxygen to give full effect to the combustion of the sulphur and carbon, making these ingredients highly inflammable when mixed together and ignited. What, though, was so special about this mixture? Petroleum, after all, which was well known in ancient warfare, is highly inflammable too. The point about saltpetre, however, is that when it reaches about 75% of the mixture, combustion becomes so fast that, when confined, it produces an actual explosion capable, among other things, of driving a projectile from a tube.

The Chinese military engineers were extremely interested in incendiary devices, but could never have discovered saltpetre themselves, and to understand how it came to be included in the gunpowder recipe we have to go to the Taoist alchemists. In the first millennium AD they were attempting to find elixirs that when drunk would prolong life and even confer immortality. Gold, and a number of other metals and minerals were central to this project, and their use in Chinese medicine was already ancient. One of the properties of saltpetre that greatly interested the alchemists is that, when combined with many metals and minerals, it converts them into salts that are soluble in water, and so can be drunk as elixirs. Saltpetre occurs naturally, as white crystals produced by the decay of organic matter such as excreta, especially in warm, humid climates. But it has to be distinguished from the sodium, calcium, and magnesium nitrates, which resemble it, and the basic test was to heat it on charcoal where it burns with a distinctive purple flame.

The alchemists, in their experiments, were always heating different mixtures, and by 300 AD are known to have heated saltpetre, sulphur, and charcoal together. In around 850 AD Tao Tsang warned alchemists not to heat saltpetre, sulphur, and honey together (honey would have produced carbon), because the result could be a devastating fire that might burn down the laboratory. The special properties of the saltpetre, sulphur, and carbon mixture, when ignited, had by now become familiar as the "fire-drug", *huo yao*, and the Taoist alchemists had social links with the military engineers. These took up the fire-drug because of the tradition of incendiary warfare in China, and its first military uses were in bamboo tubes, in the tenth century, to produce the firelance. The gunpowder it contained was not a high explosive mixture, but more like a rocket composition, shooting out powerful flames. But now that the significance of saltpetre was known it did not take the military engineers very long to discover, doubtless by trial and error, that increasing its proportion in the mixture would produce an explosive, and the first Chinese guns appeared in about 1280 AD.

Trial and error clearly played a part, then, in the discovery of gunpowder, but only in the context of some highly focused activities, and it would have been quite impossible for the Chinese to have discovered it by randomly mixing all the substances known to them. It was the multiple properties of saltpetre that were crucial here, and the different parties who were interested in them: the alchemists were initially interested in it because of its importance in preparing elixirs, and only later discovered its importance for combustion, but this property was highly relevant to the incendiary interests of military engineers.

So far, however, we have been discussing innovation in complex literate civilisations which have very rich cultural traditions and practices to draw upon in this combinatorial fashion, but the situation is very different in primitive societies. The problem with traditional crafts as a source of innovation, certainly at the village level of production, is how unexperimental and conservative they tend to be. They simply have to produce standard articles, and in this situation there is no incentive for the craftsman to spend much time exploring different possibilities that may turn out to be a waste of effort and materials.

Once people have devised something that works reasonably well, the natural temptation is to rest on one's laurels and go no further, unless there is a compelling reason to do so. This is certainly true of the history of technology, which in pre-modern societies had a very strong tendency to settle down into what we may call the "adaptive rut" once people had absorbed some new device. Why, then, should people ever leave it?

The first question a Darwinian asks himself in trying to explain why a particular custom, or institution, or belief was selected is "What *use* does it have?" Darwinian theory itself arose from a utilitarian and materialist view of man, always competing for scarce resources, and who is driven by a fundamentally animal agenda of mating, parenting, and trying to increase the proportion of his genes in the population. Our physical needs have priority over all others, which is why material factors such as population growth, geography, the modes of production, and the need to harness energy have really determined the course of history. Ideas and beliefs are little more than the reflections of social organisation and material needs, mere froth on the surface of reality, while ritual, religion, magic, and other forms of superstition are only significant for the contribution they make to social solidarity or individual self-confidence.

Technology, however, has often needed the stimulus of *non-practical motives*, such as aesthetics, intellectual curiosity, magic and religion, pride and status, or entertainment, that will encourage people to focus their attention on physical objects, and play around with them in ways that they would never think of in the ordinary work of daily life, or in relation to material needs. If early man had simply been concerned with material calculations of profit and loss and what would be immediately useful, with sober matter-of-fact and ignoring the fanciful and imaginative, then I do not think that very much would have happened at all in the way of social and cultural evolution. One fundamental reason for this is that some of the most important innovations in history had no obvious practical pay-off in their initial stages, and another reason is that primitive man often had very different ideas from us about how to *be* practical. Of course he wanted health and prosperity just as we do, but from the earliest times of which we have any reliable evidence, we know that Man did not see the world only in terms of its immediately obvious physical properties, but also as permeated by supernatural forces and beings on which his survival and prosperity depended.

Here we must remember that the environment can be, to some extent, what people think it is, and this may have no basis in objective reality. The environment is not some neutral physical space which has the same properties for all the different organisms inhabiting it, but is also defined by the specific relationships which the different organisms have with it, and has different constraints and opportunities for each of them, depending on how each of them lives. And in the case of human beings their life intimately involves *thinking* about their environment and interacting with it in ways that partially depend on how they define it.

Nature does not, however, always rap us over the knuckles whenever we get something wrong, like thinking the earth is flat; on the contrary, it can hide behind mask upon mask of ambiguity and deception. Since many different, and false, interpretations of nature will therefore all seem to work, the materialist belief that they will be eliminated by natural selection cannot be right, and mediocre ideas will survive just as well as mediocre institutions. Plants will grow perfectly well without the use of garden magic, the rain will fall without rituals to bring it, and the Aztecs did not need to slaughter thousands of human victims to ensure the survival of the sun. But for primitive man, water, air, fire and earth, animals and trees were not just physical objects but filled with mysterious powers that were akin to Man himself, so that his sexual acts and his killing of animals and men resonated with cosmic significance. Play and myths and rituals were all part of this world of the imagination, which clothed the natural world in symbolic forms, and which found expression in art, ritual, and the decoration of the body.

Disconcertingly, however, for utilitarians and materialists, these fanciful preoccupations had great practical consequences, for precisely because they inspired people to do things which were not immediately useful, they led them to explore the properties of the world around them, and so to discover the easiest pathways into its evolutionary potential. There is a popular belief, for example, that as soon as our ancestors became aware of metals, they must have seen at once that they would make much better tools and weapons than stone. In Papua New Guinea, for example, and in Polynesia, where metal was unknown in the traditional technology, the highly developed iron and steel tools of the European navigators were indeed the most eagerly sought-after of all their goods and rapidly displaced stone tools. In fact, however, our prehistoric ancestors had taken stone technology to a very high level of excellence, whereas the gold, copper, and iron they would initially have found in their pure or "native" state would have been useless for practical purposes, being softer and blunter than flint, and also required the development of a whole new technology. So why did our Neolithic ancestors bother with metals at all? It is only because gold and copper are beautiful and rare that people initially treasured them, and were sufficiently motivated to explore their properties further. In the words of R. J. Forbes, "Metal made its first impression as a fascinating luxury, from which evolved a need" (1971:10). It was man's aesthetic sense, his love of self-decoration, and his desire to own rare and precious objects that was responsible for the early development of metallurgy and of glass as well, long before their practical possibilities became obvious.

But while the earliest use of metals was for trivial purposes of personal adornment, like the shells of South Sea Islanders, unlike shells they had enormous evolutionary potential. Initially, this was in a vast range of tools and weapons, and then machines, and this potential has only been fully realised in the last few centuries by the technologies of steam and electricity which would be impossible without metal. It was only because men were willing literally to play about with these materials for the non-practical purpose of decorating their bodies, that they eventually came to understand their practical possibilities. Honour and status have also been immensely important motivations, especially in economics and warfare, which have stimulated people to efforts that mere physical survival would never have done.

For example, the first watches, such as those of Peter Henlein of Nuremburg in 1505, had primitive movements and were terrible time-keepers, losing hours every day. How, then did they survive long enough in order to be radically improved over the next two or three hundred years? The answer is that, gilded and bejewelled, and chiming the hours, they were simply "bling" for the very wealthy, worn for ostentation and not really for telling the time at all. Still today luxury mechanical watches which vary a few seconds a day can command vastly higher prices than cheap quartz watches that vary only a few seconds a month for exactly the same reason of their cultural prestige.

As societies became more complex, the importance of the non-practical as the basis of the practical did not diminish. Religion was the main inspiration for all the monumental architecture of the ancient civilisations (apart from defensive fortifications). The pyramids, for example, were of no practical use; they were huge because this appealed to the human imagination, and flattered the grandiose claims of the pharaohs, but because they were huge men learnt far more about how to build in stone and to organise great public works than if they had been content with small buildings of mud-brick. Magic, again, was to be the basis of alchemy which, among the Chinese, Arabs, and Europeans led to intense investigations into the properties of a wide range of substances in the search for the Elixir of Life that would confer immortality, and be the means of turning base metals into gold. But without these vast and deluded researches modern chemistry would not have developed.

Simple farmers all over the world observe the sun, moon, and stars as part of their general calculations about sowing and harvesting, and early navigators also used them. But the really systematic astronomical observations by the ancient civilisations went far beyond these limited practical needs, and were based on the belief that the well-ordered society had to be in tune with the heavens. A key feature of ancient astronomy was the motion of the planets which have no practical relevance whatever, unlike the sun, moon, and the fixed stars. But because they move between the constellations during the year, they were regarded as *omens*, and it was for this reason, and not some abstract interest in physical science, that the Babylonians were keeping records of their movements by 2000 BC, and it was this knowledge that the Greeks inherited. It seemed obvious to them that the earth was stationary and that it was the heavenly bodies that moved, but Aristotle taught that the heavenly bodies were spheres because they were perfect, and that circular motion was therefore natural to spheres as well. But there were some basic problems with the motion of the planets: their brightness changes during the year, and they also appear to reverse their motion from time to time, both of which are incompatible with the idea that they revolve around the earth in circular orbits.

The effort to explain the planetary motions on the basis that the earth, and not the sun, is at the centre of the universe, culminating in Ptolemy's *Almagest*, required some ingenious geometry with epicycles[6] and other devices, but in the sixteenth century Copernicus, a Catholic priest and an expert mathematical astronomer (Kuhn 1957:135–84), was asked by the Pope to correct the Julian calendar. (His calculations were later used to produce the reformed Gregorian calendar, but re-forming the calendar did not require any knowledge of how the solar system works, only more accurate astronomical observations.) He was thoroughly familiar with the *Almagest*, and with a great deal of subsequent astronomical work, but in the thirteen centuries that had passed since Ptolemy had composed the *Almagest* his calculations had accumulated many inaccuracies, and Copernicus was also extremely critical of the epicycles and other geometrical complexities of the Ptole-maic model of the solar system. He was much influenced by Neo-Platonism, and it therefore seemed to him that the Sun, the "mind", the "ruler" of the universe, which Hermes Trismegistos (the ancient and mythical originator of alchemy) called a living god, should actually be at its centre. Since God must have designed a perfect universe, He would have based the movements of the heavenly bodies on perfect circles because this was their natural motion, so Ptolemy's elaborate systems of epicycles had to be wrong. He therefore revived ancient Greek theories that the sun, not the earth, is the centre of the universe, and this also required the earth, like all spheres, not only to have a circular motion around the sun, but to rotate on its axis. How likely is it, Copernicus asks, that the whole universe could rotate around the earth in twenty-four hours, since the vast distances of the stars would involve their travelling at an unimaginable speed to achieve this? As the shore seems to be moving when seen from a ship in motion, so it is possible that the apparent motion of the heavenly bodies is actually the result of the earth's motion.

Once we think of the earth as also orbiting the sun among the other planets, the major peculiarities of planetary motion—the fact that they seem to reverse their motion, or retrogress, during part of the year, and that they vary in brightness—can easily be explained by the fact that the earth periodically overtakes the outer planets in their orbits round the sun, and is itself overtaken by the inner planets. Retrogression only occurs when this is happening, and it is also at this time that the earth is nearest to the planet in question, which is why it is also at its brightest. This was an enormous intellectual simplification of planetary motions, which had great aesthetic appeal to many scientists of the day. But there were other problems that this simple model could not solve, such as the fact that the sun moves more quickly between the autumnal and the vernal equinoxes than in the rest of the year. To account for this, and for other irregularities of the planets, Copernicus in fact had to go back again to Ptolemy's geometrical complexities, and eventually produced a system that was just as complicated as Ptolemy's and no more accurate in predicting planetary motions.

Johannes Kepler was another Neo-Platonist and Pythagorean, and a mystic and astrologer, who had been converted to Copernicanism in his student days. In 1600 he became Tycho Brahe's assistant in Prague, and gained access to his vast accumulation of very accurate observations on planetary movements. Brahe had asked him to solve the irregularities of the Martian orbit, which were the most perplexing of all the planets. As a Platonist he was convinced that the cosmos had to be based on simple mathematical principles, and as a result of studying Brahe's data he realised that the planets do not move in circular but in elliptical orbits. This explained why planets will appear from earth to move faster when they are closer to the sun than when they are farther away. On this basis it was now possible to explain all those irregularities of planetary motion that had, until then, had been insoluble on the assumption of circular orbits.

But whether the sun revolves around the earth or vice versa has been of no practical relevance until the space age of the twentieth century. The driving interest in explaining the movements of the planets throughout all the previous centuries was essentially philosophical and religious, and it is hard to imagine anyone approaching astronomy from a more "other-worldly" perspective than Copernicus and Kepler. Cultural evolution in earlier epochs has therefore been possible partly because "fanciful" beliefs like alchemy and astrology lift cultures out of the adaptive rut, and also, instead of weeding out everything that is not immediately useful, societies carry a good deal of "dead wood" that may be of no particular adaptive value at the moment. They operate rather like those people who never throw anything away, because "you never know when it may be useful".

In the neo-Darwinian model, the function of the environment is in *selecting* the variants that are produced by mutation, which is the only possible creative source. But people, unlike genes, can be deliberately creative through thought, so a constructivist theory takes a very different view of the cultural environment, which is that there are cultural environments that stimulate creativity, and others that inhibit it. One of the best refutations of the mutation and selection model of invention is the very well-known phenomenon of more or less simultaneous invention—such as calculus, logarithms, the telephone, the light-bulb, and the jet engine, but also the theory of natural selection itself. This was first published by Patrick Matthew in 1831, then in 1859 by A. R. Wallace and Darwin. All these discoveries were made by people working in basically the same culture, so naturally a number of people could all be thinking along the same lines and passing ideas around, but the idea of an environment that fosters innovation, rather than one that merely selects, can of course have no place in Darwinian thinking. While one can't predict discoveries before they are made, or invent something to order, it is certainly much easier to discover and invent in some social environments than others, where long-distance trade brings in new ideas, where there are opportunities to play about with things, where attention is focused on something as a problem, where there is literacy, where there are high levels of communication especially through printing, and where innovation is rewarded financially and admired.

What is meant by "a creative environment" is very well conveyed by the contrast between technological and scientific innovation in the ancient world and in early modern Europe. This was very much a non-linear process in which social organisation, cultural values and the conceptual understanding of nature all played essential parts. Technology is not just a set of responses to human needs, and our biological needs do not exert a constant pressure to invent. As in primitive society, even in the ancient world there was a strong tendency for technology to stagnate: "Technical progress, economic growth, productivity, even efficiency have not been significant goals since the beginning of time. So long as an acceptable life-style could be maintained, other values held the stage" (Finley 1973:147). As the complexity of technology increases, innovation becomes increasingly dependent on the social and cultural milieu, and on two factors in particular. The first is experimentation on nature, motivated by theory, and this will go beyond anything required by practical needs—it involves, in other words, an interaction between theoretical and craft knowledge.

In antiquity, however, there was a profound gulf between brain-work and manual labour, between theoretical and practical knowledge. Manual labour was despised, and craft knowledge could only be acquired by years of practical, hands-on experience in the workshop, and in this sort of apprenticeship book learning would have been irrelevant. The knowledge of literate high culture, however, especially philosophy, acquired from books, was speculative, self-consciously intellectual and concerned with the general nature of things rather than with practical detail. Natural philosophy was not intended to be useful and had very little connection with technology, which developed almost entirely at the craft level.

The second factor is cost, because any advanced form of technology is expensive, and technology cannot build itself. It requires investment, and decisions about what to invest in will be taken by a very small minority, notably rulers and rich men. Their decisions will reflect their own interests and values, and rulers favoured military technology and entertaining gadgets. For example:

> *...the Ptolemies founded and financed the Museum at Alexandria, for two centuries the main western centre of scientific research and invention. Great things emerged from the Museum, in military technology and in ingenious mechanical toys. But no one, not even the Ptolemies themselves, who would have profited directly and handsomely, thought to turn the energy and inventiveness of a Ctesibius to agricultural and industrial technology. The contrast with the Royal Society in England is inescapable (Finley 1971:148).*

Landowners in the ancient world had no need to patronise technology, and while rich men were another potential source of investment, in the ancient civilisations generally the status of merchants was rather low. Wealth was legitimated by participation in state institutions, and the pillars of the state were the king, the priesthood or some equivalent body, the landowning nobility that normally had military functions as well, the army, and provincial governors and other senior officials. Merchants were outsiders in relation to the state, and their wealth was individual, private profit which had no social function at all and was spent for purely personal gratification. Making profits by trade was often regarded as contemptible, especially by comparison with glorious military exploits, and also as probably dishonest. In the Roman Empire, for example, while obviously businessmen wanted to become rich, if they were successful they typically invested their wealth in landed estates or public benefactions rather than in their businesses. While *we* can imagine water-wheels driving banks of potters' wheels, or powering blast-furnaces and trip-hammers in iron foundries, although technically feasible they would have been very expensive to develop, and the Romans did not invest capital in that way.

Modern experimental science only developed at the beginning of the seventeenth-century in Western Europe because only there and then had the necessary social and intellectual conditions accumulated in the course of the Middle Ages and the Renaissance. These were: the availability from the Islamic world of Greek natural philosophy, especially Aristotle, and the exact sciences of astronomy, optics, and statics, that provided an advanced theoretical starting point; a unique urban environment, free from the constraints of feudalism, where the merchant class had high status and in which craftsmen had unusually high social status as well, facilitating a close intellectual association between educated men, such as physicians, engineers, architects and alchemists, and artisans such as goldsmiths, printers, painters, clock- and instrument-makers, lens-grinders, and so on, in an experimental milieu, and a milieu in which profits could be made from clocks, navigational instruments, telescopes, vacuum-pumps, etc.; where there was a fair degree of mathematical knowledge among the artisan class as well as the educated and a growing familiarity with quantification and measurement in society generally; and, notably, a prosperous and vigorous capitalist society, and commerce was largely unrestricted by arbitrary government controls and taxation. All these factors combined to provide the necessary conditions for the emergence of modern science in Western Europe with the experiments of Galileo, in particular. A further factor was political fragmentation, which prevented any one authority having the power to censor ideas, as had existed in the Chinese, Byzantine and Islamic empires:

> *The history of the Middle Ages ... leaves us, above all, with a sense of the extraordinary vigour and creativity which derives from the fragmentation of power and wealth into innumerable centres, competing and expanding into different and unexpected directions. The places where political fragmentation was most complete, such as Tuscany, the Low Countries, and the Rhineland, were perhaps the most creative. That division of authority was caused partly by small political units, partly by the overlapping of royal power, independent cities, strong seigneurs, and finally ecclesiastical authority. Hence the multifarious creativity of medieval Europeans (Holmes 1992:x).*

7. Cultural evolution and historical inevitability

Once we base our evolutionary model on self-organisation and human selection, a number of major changes in the evolutionary model follow automatically: the populational model of evolutionary change is replaced by that of structural transformation, in which some factors have special importance, a feature that the populational model is unable to capture at all. With the disappearance of the population model the need to look for those will o' the wisps, the units of culture, vanishes as well. The only kind of selection that now concerns us is human selection, and the place of natural selection is taken by self-organisation, a process not under human direction which proceeds by its own principles. Instead of adaptive explanations, with all their confusions, we look instead for the causes of innovation and change and how their effects come about. It is noteworthy that historians, political scientists, and economists never resort to adaptive explanations but always to causal explanations, unless the adaptive explanations are based on conscious choice, as for example in the adoption of breech-loading artillery or the introduction of limited liability companies.

There is a long-standing debate as to whether the process of cultural evolution implies the notion of historical inevitability. A somewhat similar idea in biology is known as "orthogenesis", "A steady trend of evolution in a given direction over a prolonged period of time, affecting related groups of organisms, due to the working out of inherent trends within the inherited material" (Abercrombie *et al.* 1973:204). Julian Huxley commented: "Most biologists … look askance at orthogenesis, in its strict sense, as implying an inevitable grinding out of results pre-determined by some internal germinal clockwork. This too much akin to vitalism and mysticism for their liking: it removes evolution out of the field of analysable phenomena; and it, too, goes contrary to Occam's razor in introducing a new and unexplained mechanism when known agencies would suffice" (Huxley 1974:465).

A basic source of confusion here has been the use of the word "direction", because we naturally think of this in terms of motion of some sort *towards* a goal or destination. In this sense the idea of cultural or biological evolution as "goal seeking" would indeed involve mystical or vitalistic ideas. While an organism can reasonably be said to be programmed with the goal of maturation to its adult form, there is no parallel either in biological or cultural evolution to the notion of the "adulthood" of species or societies. But there is another way of looking at "direction" which is not "towards a goal" but "away from a starting point", without committing ourselves about any endpoint of the process, and from this perspective there is certainly such a thing as orthogenesis in cultural evolution. We have seen how a series of key innovations such as agriculture → fixed settlements/larger communities/property owning kin groups + seniority of birth + religious functions → hierarchical social structures/inherited political office/mediation → increasing social size + trade + warfare → the state, and all that implies. The "→" only means "increases the probability of", or "facilitates" and all these factors interact with one another, but some cumulative, probabilistic process of this kind seems clearly to have operated which can be called facultative or permissive. As I said originally, "By the beginning of the Common Era, in a number of independent and unrelated parts of the world, literate civilisations with very large populations had evolved with a fairly standard set of institutions: sacred hereditary kings; a nobility; professional armies; urban civilisation and a market economy with highly developed crafts; writing; bureaucracy; priests or their equivalents; monumental architecture; and a particular interest in calendrical science and astronomy, so that the Chinese, Indians, Persians, Egyptians, Europeans, and Central Americans would have found many fundamental similarities in each other's societies." In these cases there has clearly been a similar direction of change although only a minority of societies developed this far spontaneously. Their influence then spread in a different way to pre-state societies by conquest or imitation.

But this has nothing to do with "historicism" as defined by Popper, who said, "I mean by 'historicism' an approach to the social sciences which assumes that *historical prediction* is their principal aim, and that this aim is attainable by discovering the 'rhythms' or the 'patterns', the 'laws' or the 'trends' that underlie the evolution of history" (Popper 1957:3). And Popper is also clearly right when he says that it is impossible to predict the future course of history since among other things this must be strongly influenced by scientific discovery. Since it is inherently impossible to predict what scientific discoveries will be made in the future, we therefore cannot predict what the future course of human history will be either (ibid., ix–x). But the whole model of cultural evolution which I have set up is inherently probabilistic and facultative, not in any way deterministic. To this extent it certainly makes sense to say that, given the potentialities of human beings, the properties of social organisation, and the existence of domesticable plants and animals, the emergence of the state and advanced civilisations was very likely at some times and places. If we imagine running the whole process over again (in other words, eliminating all the accidents of history), I believe the end result would still look much the same, at least in its broad outline.

Notes

1. It might have been expected that towns with the most relationships would have had a greater chance of forming nuclear alliances, but in the three games there appeared to be no correlation between the number of relationships a town had with the number of nuclear alliances in which it was involved. For example, B, G, and L were all involved in 3 nuclear alliances, but their respective relationships were 6, 11, and 5. On the other hand H, with 7 relationships, was not a member of any nuclear alliances, whereas M, with 4 relationships, was a member of 2.

2. In case it may be thought that my endorsement of complexity and self-organisation has been influenced by recent developments in biology, particularly by the work of Kauffman and the Santa Fe Institute, I would like to say that, apart from my fieldwork, the major influence occurred when I was a Post-Doctoral Fellow at Dalhousie University in 1968–70, and 1972–3. I worked in particular with my colleague David Elliott on the simulation of so-cial institutions by computer, and also became familiar with graph theory and the work of von Bertalanffy on general systems theory. My 1970 paper on alliance formation between Konso towns is an example of this research. A further influence was the work of Piaget in the 1970s. It is nevertheless very gratifying to see that the ideas of complexity and self-organisation are now in the mainstream of modern biology.

3. "An aspect very characteristic of the dynamic order in organis-mic processes can be termed *equifinality*. Processes occurring in

machine-like structures follow a fixed pathway. Therefore the final state will be changed if the initial conditions or the course of processes is altered. In contrast, the same final state, the same 'goal', may be reached from different initial conditions and in different pathways in organismic processes" (von Bertalanffy 1971:139).

4. Prof. Bruce Trigger, personal communication

5. A full account of the invention of the mechanical escapement can be found at North 2005:175–85, and Robertson 1931:14–19 also gives an earlier explanation of the escapement as based on an alarm mechanism. In the Whipple Museum of Science in Cambridge there is a working replica of Richard of Wallingford's clock, in which the striking mechanism and the escapement both operate in exactly the same way, in the manner described by North.

6. The epicycle involved two circular orbits, as shown:

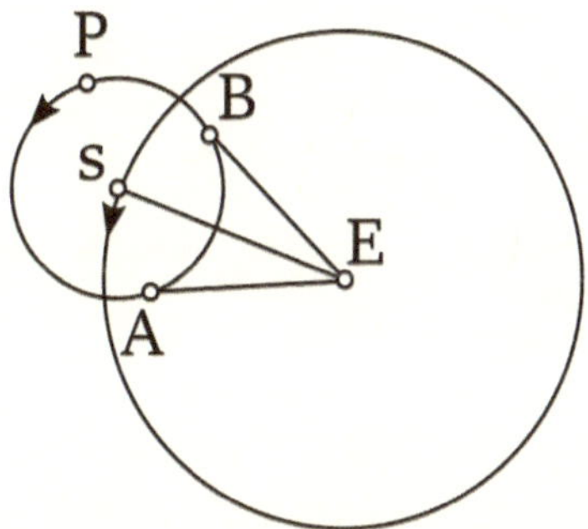

The planet P is on the small circle, the epicycle, and revolves around its centre at S; S is located on a second circle, the deferent, which has its centre at E, the earth. So the point S revolves around the earth, while the planet itself revolves around S. This epicyclic model can explain retrograde motion quite easily: to an observer on earth E, P will first seem to be moving in one direction (anti-clockwise in the diagram), but when it comes towards

A it will slow down and then seem to stop, and from A to B will seem to move in the opposite direction. The retrograde motion will also take place while the planet is closest to the earth, and therefore when it is brightest. This model of planetary motion is extremely flexible, because an endless range of different sizes of epicycle and deferent, and different relative speeds, can be devised to take account of all the variations in planetary motion.

Chapter III
Cultural evolution and sociobiology

The constructivist theory of cultural evolution that I am advocating is based on the ideas of self-organisation and human selection. So far we have been emphasising self-organisation, and we must now think in more detail about the human nature which underlies human selection. Mainstream cultural anthropology has maintained for years that there is no such thing as human nature, and that culture determines everything about what we do and think, but it should be obvious that the vast process of social evolution could not have occurred at all unless human beings had already acquired a distinctive set of characteristics through our biological evolution. Our remarkable cognitive abilities are obviously evolved traits which are basic to human society and culture, and the enormously complex societies we have constructed would also not be possible unless we were profoundly social and co-operative in nature despite also being selfish, deceitful, and competitive. Although we are easily aroused to hostility towards outsiders and readily engage in revenge and warfare, these types of behaviour are a natural response in defence of our kin and community. Gender differences will have a major influence on many areas of cultural life, from the division of labour and participation in politics and warfare, the public sphere dominated by men and the domestic by women, to the organisation of kinship and marriage, and the allocation of religious roles. Again, there are common forms of thought and belief, such as dualistic thinking, myth, ritual, and magic, and some form of cosmology which are universal, suggesting that they are expressions of innate psychological dispositions. There is also a whole range of universal social institutions such as marriage and the family, kin groups, property, reciprocity and exchange, rites of passage, status differences, and division of labour by age and gender, music, singing and dancing, a love of power and status and of bodily adornment and luxury articles, and sexual and excretory modesty, that are rooted more broadly in our human nature (Brown 1991:130–41), despite all the attempts by cultural anthropologists to deny these obvious facts.

These general characteristics of human nature have clearly exerted a powerful influence on cultural evolution, but Tooby and Cosmides, Pinker and other sociobiologists[1] go much further. They maintain that our ancestors in East Africa during the Pleistocene developed highly specialised areas of the brain, or "mental modules" to solve the various problems of survival that faced them, and it is to these biological characteristics of the individual that we must look for the basis of cultural evolution. According to E. O. Wilson, the founder of sociobiology, "Despite the imposing holistic traditions of Durkheim in sociology and Radcliffe-Brown in anthropology, cultures are not superorganisms that evolve by their own dynamics. Rather, cultural change is the statistical product of the separate behavioural responses of large number of human beings who cope as best they can with social existence" (Wilson 2004:78), and as Richard Alexander says, "[H]uman behaviour must be studied as the outcome of the interactions of individuals" (1979:48). So let's begin by putting this claim to the test straight away, before we consider what problems our prehistoric ancestors may, or may not, have faced during the Pleistocene.

1. Individualistic explanations for social institutions

It is obvious and trivial that only individual human beings can actually make things happen in a society, but what they do and think is also the expression of their position in the social and cultural scheme of things. The case of Konso town alliances showed very clearly that individuals operate within a much larger network of ties and relationships, so that social organisation could not possibly be just "the statistical product of the separate behavioural responses of large numbers of human beings". If it were, how, for instance, could Wilson and Alexander explain one of the most obvious features of both agrarian and modern industrial states, which is that a very small minority of the social elite typically owns most of the wealth, whereas the great majority of the people own very little. For example, after the Norman conquest, out of an English population of between 1½ and 2 million, William the Conqueror kept about a fifth of the land for himself, gave a quarter to the Church, and divided the rest among 170 "tenants-in-chief", or barons, as a reward for their support at the Battle of Hastings. In case this is thought to be a medieval aberration, it has been estimated that the eight richest men in the world own as much as the poorest half of the world's population, about three and a half billion people. Rather obviously, the "separate behavioural responses of large numbers of human beings" can hardly have been aimed at reducing themselves to poverty and making a few nobles or company directors extremely rich, and it is indeed the *systemic properties* of feudal society and global capitalism that were actually responsible. Whether Wilson likes it or not, cultures *are* a kind of superorganism.

We can provide a much more precise test of the sociobiologists' claim that social institutions have to be explained as the outcome of individual motives and behaviour, which are themselves governed by Darwinian imperatives of striving for reproductive success. In some societies benefits which would normally be given by the father to his children are given instead to his sister's children. Favouring one's sister's children rather than one's own, however, is the opposite strategy to that which inclusive fitness theory would predict, and R. D. Alexander (1979:168) says that this is one of "the most provocative and outstanding apparent contradictions of an evolutionary view of human behaviour". His explanation is that when a man's *confidence of paternity* reaches a sufficiently low level, his investment in his sister's children will be a significantly better bet than investment in his own for maximising inclusive fitness, since for obvious reasons it is much easier to be certain of a child's mother than of its father. So, he concludes: "… a general society-wide lowering of confidence of paternity *will lead to* [my emphasis] a society-wide prominence, or institutionalisation, of mother's brother as an appropriate male dispenser of paternal benefits" (ibid., 172).

Gaulin and Schlegel (1980) proposed the hypothesis that: "High paternal confidence leads to high investment by a man in his wife's children; low paternal confidence leads a man to channel his investment elsewhere" (ibid., 304). Where, exactly? They propose that rules for the inheritance of real and movable property, succession to the office of local headman, residence rules, and modes of reckoning descent may all be expressions of mother's brother's investment, and they have summarised their conclusions in Table 1 below (ibid., 305):

Table 1: Investment patterns and paternal confidence

Investment patterns	Low paternal confidence	High paternal confidence	χ^2	p
Residence	matrilocal, avunculocal, uxorilocal	patrilocal, virilocal, neolocal	7.783	0.005
Inheritance of real property	no fixed rules, sister's son, other matrilineal	sons, children, other patrilineal	6.599	0.010
Inheritance of movable property	no fixed rules, sister's son, other matrilineal	sons, children, other patrilineal	5.146	0.023
Descent system	matrilineal	patrilineal, bilateral	2.784	0.095
Succession to office of local headman	sister's son, other matrilineal non-hereditary	sons, other patrilineal	2.618	0.106

The aggregate of p [probability] = 0.00000001, and the authors conclude: "It seems unlikely that we are looking at a chance association" (ibid., 306). It does indeed, but is this association what the authors think it is? It will be seen from Table 1 that there is a clear tendency for low paternal confidence to be associated with matrilocal residence and matrilineal inheritance of property, office, and the reckoning of descent and, conversely, for high paternal confidence to accompany patrilocality and patrilineal inheritance and descent reckoning. So what the authors have really been doing is simply to explicate the social structure of matrilineal versus patrilineal descent groups in general, and of matrilocality versus patrilocality (and its variants) in particular.

We are dealing, then, with the social consequences of matrilocal residence, and of matrilineal descent *groups* in general as indicators of what are likely to be the relations between the sexes and especially between husbands and wives. Since in traditional societies men exercise authority over women and not *vice versa*, matrilineal descent groups will face a dilemma that does not occur for patrilineal descent groups. As Schneider has said, whereas patrilineal descent groups can allow their women to pass outside their control at marriage and into the exclusive control of their husbands, men of matrilineal descent groups must continue to retain control over their women after marriage if the corporate existence of the descent group is to be maintained since membership in the group passes through these women. Thus "The institutionalisation of very strong, lasting, or intensive solidarity between husband and wife is not compatible with maintenance of matrilineal descent groups" (Schneider 1961:16), and "There is always potential conflict between the bonds of marriage and descent; given exogamy, they are bonds which cannot coincide but pull each party to a marriage in different directions" (ibid., 17). Because in this system of relations a man has only limited control over his wife, women have greater social freedom, and it is likely that this will also involve greater sexual freedom in many such societies. This is why there may well be a lower level of paternal confidence in the matrilineal situation than in the patrilineal one, but the greater "investment" of males in their sisters' children will be the consequence of the matrilineal kinship system, not of low paternal confidence. In other words, it is the matrilineal kinship system which is the source *both* of the avunculate and of the lowered confidence in paternity.

Nor, in addition, is there any reason to suppose that merely because in some of these societies a brother makes formal gifts to his sister and her children, or leaves his property to them, their reproductive chances are thereby increased by comparison with those of his own children, or that any sacrifice of an altruistic nature by the mother's brother is involved either (for details see Hallpike 1984:141–2).

This analysis of the avunculate is just one illustration of the point that social institutions cannot be directly related to any specific strategies or purposes of individuals, such as lowered confidence of paternity, proposed by inclusive fitness theorists, because social systems have properties of their own that are not reducible to the motives and actions of individuals. Rodney Needham's *Structure and Sentiment* (1962) makes exactly the same point. It was a response to the theory proposed by Homans and Schneider that preferential marriage of a man to the daughter of his mother's brother was because of the mother's brother's affection for his nephew, whereas Needham showed that it was actually produced by the working of the whole system of kinship and marriage.

2. The environment of evolutionary adaptation

Sociobiologists argue that since we are (undoubtedly) physical organisms, that have evolved like all animals by the operation of natural selection over millions of years, therefore "Human minds, human behaviour, human artifacts, and human culture are all biological phenomena—aspects of the phenotypes of humans and their relationships with one another" (Tooby and Cosmides 1992:20–21). The emergence and evolution of human culture is therefore only a continuation of the earlier evolution of life in general with all its chemical and biological processes, and not in any way different or discontinuous from what has preceded it. Indeed, theorists like Tooby and Cosmides believe that Darwinism has to be extended to human society in order to unify the natural and human sciences, and that without this step the validity of Darwinism itself could be challenged. "In this vast landscape of causation, it is now possible to locate 'Man's place in nature' to use Huxley's famous phrase, and therefore to understand for the first time what humankind is and why we have the characteristics that we do" (ibid., 20).

This is therefore a fundamentally materialist view of Man which has no place for the mind as traditionally understood. "The rise of computers and, in their wake, modern cognitive science, completed the conceptual unification of the mental and physical worlds by showing how physical systems can embody information and meaning" (ibid., 20). They therefore approach the topic of cultural evolution from a rather different perspective than that of Universal Darwinism because they think that the human mind and human nature are products of evolutionary developments during our ancestry in East Africa, during which our brains developed in very particular ways to solve the problems of survival during the Pleistocene epoch. These evolved human characteristics then shaped subsequent cultural evolution in ways that we shall examine.

But if one is claiming that the traits of any species are adaptations to a particular environment, it is obviously rather important to know in some detail what that environment is like (Hallpike 2011d). The difficulty for the evolutionary psychologists is that we know virtually nothing about the details of the Environment of Evolutionary Adaptation (EEA) and how our ancestors coped with this environment. Even in the case of the earliest *Homo sapiens sapiens* from around 200,000 years ago we do not know if they had the ability to speak, and if so, what sort of things they might have said to each other, what made them laugh, what they quarrelled about or how they maintained peaceful relations within the group. Nor do we have any idea when they first had personal names, or when they could form the ideas of "mother's brother", or a lineage, or when they developed the idea of some sort of official union between adult men and women, or if they exchanged women between bands, or how hunting co-operation was organised, or what sort of leadership existed. Nor do we know when Man first had ideas of magic and symbolism, gods, ghosts, and spirits, or when or why he first performed religious rituals and disposed of the dead in a more than merely physical manner.

Secondly, if such mental modules had really evolved through natural selection they could only be adept in solving the kinds of problem that would have presented themselves in the conditions of the EEA, and we can at least be sure that these would have been vastly less demanding than those of modern industrial civilisation. How is it then that man's extraordinary intellectual abilities are vastly greater than would have been necessary to cope with the problems he would have faced in this environment? This fundamental point about human abilities was first made by A. R. Wallace, Darwin's co-formulator of the theory of natural selection, who had extensive first-hand acquaintance with hunter-gatherers of the Amazon and south-east Asia. He noted that on the one hand their mode of life made only very limited intellectual demands on them, and did not require abstract concepts of number and geometry, space, time, music, and advanced ethical principles, yet as individuals they were potentially capable of mastering the highly demanding cognitive skills of modern industrial civilisation if they were given the chance to acquire them. Since, as noted, natural selection can only produce traits that are adapted to existing, and not future, conditions, it "could only have endowed savage man with a brain a little superior to that of an ape, where he actually possesses one little inferior to that of a philosopher" (Wallace 1871:356). But in neo-Darwinian theory biological adaptations can only be to *existing* circumstances, never to those that might be encountered in the future. The answer to this conundrum will emerge at the end of the chapter, and it is not one that the neo-Darwinists find congenial.

3. Cheating

Knowing little about contemporary primitive societies, and even less about the EEA, evolutionary psychologists have not only assumed that all social institutions must be explained as the outcome of individual motivations, but also (very rashly) assume that Darwinian theory can tell us what those motivations are. To begin with, "It has been a cardinal assumption of neo-Darwinism that co-operation in nature is a theoretical 'problem'—a phenomenon that is at odds with the basic principle of gene competition, and that extraordinary conditions are required to overcome the inherent selective bias against the evolution of co-operation" (Corning 2005:189). In the first place, then, all animals must be basically selfish, and only disposed to behave altruistically to close kin who share many of their genes—"inclusive fitness", so since Man is an animal we must be basically selfish too. Sociobiologists have therefore spilled gallons of ink in discussing how human beings ever managed to co-operate, because cheaters or free-loaders will always have a competitive advantage over altruists. The idea of inclusive fitness was one solution, and R. L. Trivers (1971) also developed the theory of "reciprocal altruism", in which the exchange of benefits between *non-kin* can also be selectively advantageous for both parties concerned. Our friends Cosmides and Tooby discuss this as follows:

> *Reciprocal altruism, or social exchange, typically involves two acts: what "you" do for "me" (act 1), and what "I" do for "you" (act 2). For example, you might help me out by baby-sitting my child (act 1), and I might help you out by taking care of your vegetable garden when you are out of town (act 2). Imagine the following the situation: Baby-sitting my child inconveniences you a bit, but this inconvenience is more than compensated for by my watering your garden when you are out of town. Similarly, watering your garden inconveniences me a bit, but this is outweighed by the benefit to me of your baby-sitting my child (1992:171).*

As they say, one might expect natural selection to favour the emergence of this type of behaviour. But, they continue:

> *...there is a hitch: You can benefit even more by cheating me. If I take care of your garden, but if you do not baby-sit my child ... then you benefit more than if we both co-operate.... Moreover, the same set of incentives applies to me. This single fact constitutes a barrier to the evolution of social exchange.... (ibid., 172).*

While, they admit, it is effectively impossible to cheat if the exchange is simultaneous, as when we give money for the goods that we purchase, "in the absence of a widely accepted medium of exchange, most exchanges are not simultaneous, and therefore do provide opportunities for defection" (ibid., 175) like the baby-sitting/garden-watering defection we first considered. As a consequence they maintain that humans must, during the Pleistocene, have evolved a cognitive "module" of phenomenal complexity (ibid., 177) in order to handle the problem of cheating while still being able to engage in social exchange.

Bearing in mind that we are supposed to be discussing the *evolution* of social exchange among early human beings, the examples of baby-sitting and garden-watering seem somewhat remote from anything our ancestors might plausibly have been doing on the African savannah during the Pleistocene. In fact the whole discussion is utterly disengaged from the actual realities of hunter-gatherer life, and is, of course, highly ethnocentric and actually located in our own comfortably familiar WEIRD (Western, Educated, Industrial, Rich, and Democratic) societies of vast towns full of strangers. In a hunter-gatherer society exchange is actually between people who know each other very well indeed, unlike the suburban baby-sitters and garden-waterers in the example, and is also dominated by *custom*, which leaves very little room for the elaborate calculations so improbably envisaged by Cosmides and Tooby. They are so obsessed with game theory, algorithms, and differential reproduction that they never think for a moment to ask the simple, practical question: "How can people continuously living in very small groups, who have all grown up together and know one another well, who have no money, and who engage in the very basic subsistence tasks of foraging and hunting, actually manage to cheat one another day after day without it being quite obvious?" And even if someone did attempt to cheat it would instantly become known and be greatly to the *disadvantage* of the cheater from the social point of view, regardless of any material benefit. It is therefore not surprising that in face-to-face societies:

> *…those individuals who follow elementary strategies of "selfishness" and "cheating", and persistently attempt to get without giving in social relations are not only rapidly detected but punished by sanctions ranging from contempt and low status to expulsion from the group or death. Correspondingly, rewards go not to the obvious spongers and cadgers and delinquents but to those who are perceived (rightly or wrongly) to contribute most to the welfare of the group (Hallpike 1984:133–4).*

The basic assumption of evolutionary psychologists that humans are fundamentally selfish is not based on actual psychological evidence, or even reading ethnographies, but is simply a dogma of neo-Darwinian theory, reinforced by the long tradition of Western individualism and the image of *Homo economicus* rationally striving to maximise his own material interests. In primitive society generally, however one of the most admired virtues is generosity, and one of the most despised vices is meanness. Among the Tauade, who are typical of Papua New Guinea, the lowest social class, the least successful, are the "rubbish-men":

> *…the* malavi *[rubbish-men] are conventionally considered mean. They are* komutuma, *people who do not give; their bellies are bitter,* lat'logivai, *as opposed to the people who give generously, the* alituma, *especially those who give to children and old people. The* malavi, *or*

those who have their nature, are also greedy, and stuff themselves with food and lick the grease from their hands, and when they have something, such as tobacco which they should share, take it away to smoke in private.... A malavi *will go and hide in the bush and try to avoid contributing to feasts in the form of pork or food (Hallpike 1977:144).*

What is completely missing from the ideas of the evolutionary psychologists is the awareness of a small *society* as a long-term working entity, a co-operative endeavour with every individual dependent on his kin and neighbours. As a result the exaggerated importance of cheating in the society of early hunter-gatherers held by evolutionary psychologists gets the whole issue back to front. Many years ago I pointed out that in primitive society generally:

...the surest method of ensuring social failure and, presumably, some corresponding decrease in inclusive fitness, is to follow simple strategies of "selfishness" or "cheating". But human society provides at least two basic means by which some individuals can enrich themselves and their relatives at the expense of other members of the group. The successful person may gain control over some crucial resource such as land or cattle, or some crucial process, such as political leadership, and use this as a basis of exploitative relations with dependent individuals, who are induced to confer more benefits on the dominant individual than the costs to him of maintaining control over them. Or, the successful person may have some ability, such as specialised knowledge, that is valued by the group [e.g. shamanism] but is in short supply, and thereby extract more benefits from the group than the cost of supplying such services (Hallpike 1984:135).

Social, and reproductive, success in primitive society, therefore, is achieved by those who are perceived to *help* the group, not by those who cheat and sponge from it. Evolutionary psychologists are obsessed for doctrinal reasons with the notion that the key threat to co-operation in human groups is the outsider, the free-loading stranger. Among hunter-gatherers strangers are a possible burden on resources, but in farming societies strangers are not a problem because resources are much richer and increased numbers are generally advantageous for co-operation in agricultural work and for security; if strangers start to be resented it is, again, because they are thought to be putting too much pressure on scarce resources, not because they are thought to be cheats. It is the people one already knows and dislikes for one reason or another that are always the threat to social cohesion.

It should actually be obvious that it is not the hunter-gatherer band but large, anonymous, wealthy societies like our own, with a high frequency of one-off transactions between strangers, where cheating will become much easier and provide by far the most favourable environment for free-loaders to flourish.

4. Human co-operation

Rather obviously, then, the image of humans as fundamentally selfish is grossly distorted. It is of course true that "All viable organisms must have a selfish streak if they are to survive. But human co-operation and helpfulness are laid on top of this self-interested foundation" (Tomasello 2009:xx). Instead of speculating about our prehistoric ancestors in East Africa during the Pleistocene, Professor Tomasello conducted comparative research at the Max Planck Institute of Evolutionary Anthropology in Leipzig, on infants of 12 to 24 months, and on chimpanzees. This confirmed that, unlike apes, "To an unprecedented degree, *Homo sapiens* are adapted for acting and thinking co-operatively in cultural groups" (ibid., xv). Inclusive fitness theorists concentrate almost entirely on gift-giving as the test of altruism, but Tomasello points out that this is far too narrow, because it is only one part of a much more comprehensive pattern of collaboration and mutual assistance, and an atmosphere of tolerance and trust, that is innate and uniquely human.

Human infants start co-operating at about a year, and when 14–18 month-old infants were put in situations where adult strangers needed help with a variety of problems, like picking up something they had dropped, or opening a cupboard door, the infants spontaneously helped them. "To help others flexibly in these ways, infants need, first, to be able to perceive others' goals in a variety of situations, and second to have the altruistic motive to help them. This behaviour emerges very early, without training. Parental rewards do not increase infant helpfulness, but actually inhibit it, and it occurs cross-culturally" (ibid., 12–13).

Again, teaching is a form of altruism, founded on a motive to help, in which individuals donate information to others for their use, and humans actively teach each other things without regard to kinship. Even before speech develops, infants will try to provide information to adult strangers who need it by pointing, but apes do not understand this type of informative pointing at all. They do sometimes point at humans, but only to indicate that they want something for themselves; on the other hand, "Confronted with pointing, [human] infants appear to ask themselves 'Why does *she* think that my attending to that cup will be helpful or relevant to *me*?'" (ibid., 18).

Very young children may offer to share, and the tendency to share increases with age, being accompanied by a rapid growth in the capacity for empathy. From the age of eighteen months on, children "understand how to hurt, comfort, or exacerbate another's pain; they understand the consequences of their hurtful actions for others and something of what is allowed or disapproved behaviour in their family world; they anticipate the response of adults to their own and others' misdeeds; and they differentiate between transgressions of various kinds" (Damon & Hart 1988:169).

Infants also have an innate grasp of rules, in the sense of readily understanding that things *should* be done in a certain way, and try to enforce this. Children therefore legislate norms by themselves, regardless of parental instruction, even when not immediately involved in an activity, so that, observing a solitary game, they will condemn a puppet who is introduced and then disobeys the rules. The notion of the ideal way of how a game ought to be played follows directly from watching an adult, and children don't need to see the adult corrected. So rules are not just instrumental guides to the children's own effective action, but are supra-individual entities that carry social force independently of instrumental considerations (ibid., 38). Children's earliest norms (at around 3 years) are therefore true social norms, and they result from something more than either the fear of authority or the promise of reciprocity. These cannot, in particular, account for the child's active enforcement of social norms, since they are not taught to do this (Tomasello 2009:39).

For this degree of co-ordination and communication to be possible, the participants must therefore have (1) a joint goal in the sense that they, in mutual knowledge, do X together, and (2) the participants must co-ordinate their roles which are interdependent, and this requires communication. Tomasello calls this form of interaction "We-mode". In the case of chimps hunting monkeys, however, while individuals are mutually responsive to one another's spatial position as they encircle the prey, each participant tries to maximise his *own* chance of catching the prey, without any prior joint goal or plan or assignment of roles. This is behaving in I-mode, not We-mode (ibid., 60–62).

Children of even one year old, however, can work in We-mode. In a series of tests with 14–24 month-old infants, the children collaborated easily in social games, but the chimps had no interest at all in the games and refused to take part in them. Researchers also engaged in collaborative activity with some very young children of about 18 months, and then exchanged roles the next time. The children easily adapted to their new roles, suggesting that they understood the adult's perspective and role. Chimps did not reverse roles in same way, only having a first-person perspective. So human collaborative activity is achieved through generalised roles potentially filled by anybody, including the self.

We are, then, innately social beings to whom co-operation comes quite naturally and this ease of collaboration and enforcement of norms is also closely connected with conformity. Humans have a tendency to imitate others in the group simply in order to be like them, that is, to conform (perhaps as an indicator of group identity). Moreover, they sometimes even invoke co-operatively agreed-upon social norms of conformity on others in the group, and their appeals to conformity are backed by various potential punishments or sanctions for those who resist. To our knowledge, no other primates collectively create and enforce group norms of conformity (Tomasello 2009:70).

The human passion for conformity, and readiness to punish those who violate it, should be obvious to everyone (especially academics), as is our extreme sensitivity to our social reputations (consider here the blushing reflex), and our susceptibility to insult.

5. The naked ape

Empirical experiments such as those of Tomasello and his colleagues reveal very basic differences between chimpanzees and humans, but one of the most cherished beliefs of the sociobiologists is how many significant aspects of human behaviour are directly inherited from our ape and even monkey ancestors. For example, after a long discussion of baboons, two sociobiologists conclude: "Human political systems are based on hierarchy and competition for status... it must be understood that the process which gives rise to empire is *the very same process* [my italics] that primates engage in simply in order to exist and persist" (Tiger & Fox 1971:2–3). According to them, apes and monkeys can therefore provide us with the "behavioural grammar" needed to understand human nature, especially power and domination. Among chimpanzees, "dominance seems almost to be an end in itself for males of this species, and... alphas and other high-ranking individuals gain reproductive benefits via political intimidation in mating and food competition" (Boehm 1999:30). Sociobiologists also think of power in very simplistic terms as mere bullying: "The type of power I have in mind is straightforwardly conceived. In its raw form it is like the power we see exhibited in groups of chimpanzees... It is the dominant's power to intimidate and take something away from someone, or to force another to do something" (ibid., 5). The problem for biologists who believe that we have simply inherited this lust for power and domination from our ape and monkey ancestors, is that ancient hunter-gatherers presumably resembled modern ones in being notably egalitarian, without any of the dominant alpha-males of the chimpanzee or baboon variety. (If any try to appear, they are rapidly put in their place.) Then, with the development of farming and more complex societies dominated by chiefs, kings, and emperors, dominance hierarchies appeared once again.

One sociobiologist, Christopher Boehm, has tried to solve this apparent problem by arguing that hunter-gatherers are just as hierarchically disposed as chimpanzees, but have discovered how to act as a group to suppress potential alpha-male bullies, in what he calls a "reverse dominance hierarchy", which was then favoured by natural selection and became an inherited trait: "It is primarily on the basis of vigilance that hunter-gatherers have kept their societies egalitarian in spite of individual tendencies that could lead to despotism. Over the long term, the result is a reverse social dominance...*with the subordinates firmly in charge*" [my emphasis] (Boehm 1999:88).

As a result, in modern democracies, too, we have the vote:

...because we want to keep a say in our own governance, but, more basically, we exert it because we are suspicious of all governance and wish to limit the powers of those who lead and may therefore try to rule... Our earliest precursor, in this respect, may well have been [!] an African ape living some 5 to 7 million years ago. This vanished ancestral hominoid was likely to have formed political coalitions that

enabled the rank and file, those who otherwise would have been ut-
terly subordinated, to whittle away at the powers of alpha individuals
whose regular practice it was to bully them (ibid., vii).

In the first place, when we are invited to speculate in this way about the political lives of "vanished ancestral hominoids", who disappeared 5 million years or so ago, and to "develop a full behavioural portrait of the Common Ancestor of the four African-based hominoids [including us]" of 7 million years ago, we are entitled to some degree of scepticism, to put it mildly. E. O. Wilson has pointed out that "Two thousand generations, roughly the time since typical *Homo sapiens* invaded Europe, is enough time to create new species and to mould their anatomy and behaviour in major ways" (Wilson 2004:91). But 5 million years gives *250,000* generations (at 20 years to the generation) which is more than 100 times as many generations as those necessary to create new species, while 7 million years gives 350,000 generations. (Baboons, indeed, are not apes at all but monkeys, and the split between these and apes occurred no less than 25 million years, or 1,250,000 generations ago!) Given these enormous evolutionary distances, how would "a full behavioural portrait" of the Common Ancestor be possible, and what relevance would it have anyway?

Modern humans, as found among hunter-gatherers, are clearly an entirely new species with a number of unique characteristics which set them quite apart from the world of apes and monkeys, in particular through their enormously enhanced cognitive and co-operative abilities:

- The modern human brain with all its formidable cognitive and imaginative powers.

- The possession of language, with profound implications for social life, such as planning, social bonding, giving information about other group members, and conveying values and social norms.

- The possession of tools and weapons that could be used for killing other people as well as animals, and therefore bad news for bullies.

- The control of fire and the cooking of food (see below).

- None of the primate competition for mates, but stable, recognised unions between males and females. The elimination of female estrus allowed frequent sexual activity that cemented this pair bonding, and also "reduced the potential for [male] competition and safeguarded the alliances of hunter males" (Wilson 2004:140–41).

- Marriage as an economic as well as a sexual relationship. Women cook food for their husbands, who provide meat and protect wives and their food (Wrangham 2009).

- None of the primate competition for food, but co-operation in hunting and systematic rules for sharing.

- A unique repertoire of behaviours such as crying with tears, disgust, and laughter.

- A long period of children's dependence on parents and adults.

These vast differences between human and primate society radically change the rules of social life from individualistic competition to group co-operation, in which the dominance hierarchies of the baboon and chimpanzee type would be quite out of place.

So the biologists' fixation on the social life of apes and monkeys, far from illuminating the basics of human nature, only serves to confuse the issue. They are guilty, in particular, of an elementary fallacy when they suppose that human social hierarchies are the same kind of thing as the dominance hierarchies of apes and monkeys. The fallacy is this: the bullying by alpha-male chimpanzees, biting, scratching, jumping up and down and screaming and waving branches, is *entirely self-serving*, with minimal concern for the welfare of the group, and is simply part of the ongoing competition between all the males for food and mates. But human social leadership and positions of authority have nothing to do with bullying of the chimpanzee variety: the notion of a leader imposing his will on his followers like an alpha-male chimpanzee misses the whole point of leadership in simple societies, which is that the leader has to attract people by having something to offer them, by being a social benefactor in some way, not by threatening them, because individuals are free to live more or less where and with whom they like, and have free access to all the necessities of life. The idea that the strongest man could simply seize control and bully all the rest of the group into submission is quite unrealistic: even the strongest man has to sleep, the other men are just as well armed, and even if such a would-be dictator were not murdered, people would simply abandon him and go and live somewhere else.

Positions of power and leadership in human societies are produced by situations in which some people control what other people want or need, like food, land, personal security, political skills, status, wealth, the favour of the gods, professional expertise, knowledge, and so on. In other words, power requires *dependency*, and among hunter-gatherers there is precious little of that, because social organisation is very simple and everyone has equal access to resources. This is why leadership roles are so muted in their type of society, not because we have inherited "a reverse-dominance hierarchy". In the more complex societies produced by agriculture and the domestication of animals, people may cease to be self-sufficient in defence, or in access to resources or to the supernatural, or a host of other things, so they will be willing to accept inequality of power because they obviously get something out of war-leaders, or clan heads, or priests. Once we understand that human social hierarchies are based on dependency, not on bullying, and are generally regarded as quite *legitimate* and in the general interest, Boehm's claim that "One of the great mysteries of social evolution is the transition from egalitarian to hierarchical society" (Boehm

1999:88) ceases to be a mystery at all, but a non-problem produced by the delusion that humans are still really apes at heart.

All that happens as societies become more complex is that the opportunities for dependency become more frequent, and that we generalise our ingrained acceptance of the authority of parents and elders to include Big Men, clan heads, nobles, and so on, ending with kings who are fathers of their people, and priests who are fathers of their flocks. Once this is understood, we can see that the social hierarchies of increasingly complex societies like chiefdoms, kingdoms, empires, and modern industrial society have nothing in common with the individualistic bullying of chimpanzee groups but are the result of complex systems of dependency, and are essential for organising large-scale societies.

6. Hypertrophy

In fairness to sociobiology it should be stated that E. O. Wilson does attempt to account for the broad features of cultural evolution from hunter-gatherers to literate civilisation, and gives what is in many ways a good summary of its basic features and the order in which they occurred (2004:88–90). As he says, "The similarities between the early civilisations of Egypt, Mesopotamia, India, China, Mexico, and Central and South America in these major features [administration, division of labour, law, religion, monumental architecture etc.] are remarkably close. They cannot be explained away as the products of chance or cultural cross-fertilisation" (ibid., 89). Indeed they can't, but his own explanation is yet another lapse into linear causal thinking: a genetically programmed unfolding of human adaptations:

In my opinion the key to the emergence of civilisation is hypertrophy, the extreme growth of pre-existing structures. Like the teeth of the baby elephant that lengthen into tusks, and the cranial bones of the male elk that sprout into astonishing great antlers, the basic social responses of the hunter-gatherers have metamorphosed from relatively modest environmental adaptations into unexpectedly elaborate, even monstrous forms in more advanced societies. Yet the directions this change can take and its final products are constrained by the genetically influenced behavioural dispositions that constituted the earlier, simpler adaptations of preliterate human beings *[my emphasis] (ibid., 89).*

So hypertrophy has applied to the subordination of women, "…the great majority of societies have evolved toward sexual domination as though sliding along a ratchet"; and "Nationalism and racism, to take two examples, are the culturally nurtured outgrowths of simple tribalism" (ibid., 92). "Most and perhaps all of the other prevailing characteristics of modern societies can be identified as hypertrophic modifications of the biologically meaningful institutions of hunter-gatherer bands and early tribal states" (ibid., 92). Child care, kin classification, the division of labour, warfare, and the sharing of knowledge are further cases in point, though religion and class structure "…are such gross transmutations that only the combined resources of anthropology and history can hope to trace their cultural phylogeny back to rudiments in the hunter-gatherers' repertory. But even these might in time be subject to a statistical characterisation consistent with biology" (ibid., 95–6).

He does at least admit the importance of cultural factors. So in discussing aggression he says, "The cultural evolution of aggression appears to be guided jointly by the following three forces: (1) genetic predisposition toward learning some form of communal aggression; (2) the necessities imposed by the environment in which the society finds itself; and (3) the previous history of the group, which biases it toward the adoption of one cultural innovation as opposed to another" (ibid., 114). From my own studies of Konso and Tauade warfare I generally agree with what Wilson says here, but it does not support his claim that "The practice of war is a straightforward example of a hypertrophied biological disposition" (ibid., 116). The capacity for physical aggression is part of human, and especially male, nature, but the motivations for warfare in tribal society and in modern industrial states have quite different patterns. Killing one's hated neighbours from across the river in revenge for their murder of one's relatives, and thereby gaining the sexual favours of the women of one's own group, has no resemblance to the motives of politicians who order soldiers in modern armies to kill complete strangers in distant countries, or to the motives of the soldiers who obey those orders. Appealing to human biology is entirely inadequate to explain these very different patterns of warfare: as one distinguished anthropologist has put it, "the reasons people fight are not the reasons wars take place" (Sahlins 1977:8). The notion of hypertrophy becomes even more inadequate when it encounters religion.

According to Wilson, "The predisposition to religious belief is the most complex and powerful force in the human mind and in all probability an ineradicable part of human nature" (ibid., 169), and "constitutes the greatest challenge to human sociobiology" (ibid., 175). It is not, in fact, a simple disposition like "belief in spiritual beings" that could plausibly be described as innate, but a highly complex phenomenon both psychologically and culturally, and there are major differences between the forms of religion found in primitive societies and the world religions.

It is also quite wrong to suppose that what we understand as "religious belief" can also be found in primitive society and is "an ineradicable part of human nature". Our belief has a cognitive component, a positive assent to certain doctrines as "true" which it is also possible to doubt or to deny, as well as the emotional element of personal experience of the divine. But while the Konso, for example, can be said to "believe" in the Sky God Waqa who brings the rain, or indeed in some sense *is* the rain, they do so in the different sense of simply taking his existence for granted without the possibility and choice of unbelief. Waqa is also "far away" and there is certainly no idea of any personal experience of him or of loving him.

In the early stages of the development of thought people certainly think most easily about causes as the actions of some kind of agent, so there is no doubt that gods or equivalent supernatural beings are an important aspect of religion at all levels of development. But when anthropologists encounter religion even in the primitive societies of hunter-gatherers and early farmers, they find it is far wider in scope than supernatural beings. These, in the form of witches, ghosts, and spirits of one kind or another have actually remained remarkably unchanged throughout history up until the present day, and it is only the notions of the divine which have radically evolved.

Members of hunter-gathering and farming societies assume they can interact by words and actions with the physical world *as if it were part of their own social world,* and this is the really important point about the early forms of religion. They are not focused on personal salvation and a Heavenly world quite different from the world of ordinary experience, but on gaining health and prosperity for themselves and their community in this world. Its rituals do not have creeds and doctrines and are a kind of public magic, the communal manipulation of sacred objects and actions to bring Life and prosperity to the *group.* Nor do they involve personal spiritual experience, such as prayer or meditation, nor the well-being of the soul.

It is also often impossible to draw a clear distinction between the religious and the social. So clans in tribal society may not be seen merely as social institutions but are often thought of as having a close, "totemic", relationship with species of birds, animals, and plants, and their founders and heads are seen as endowed with sacred powers. All over the world in myth and ritual we find a range of symbolic categories that link the social and the natural worlds: the wild and the tame; order and disorder; purity and pollution; normal and abnormal; village and bush; life and death; male and female; right and left; symbolic reversal; light and dark; and sky and earth. These are not primarily concerned with supernatural *agents* as such, but serve to embed human society in what we would call the natural world, and all such categories are expressed by a rich symbolism in ritual and myth. The gods are essentially important as beings of power, bringers of Life and death and guardians of cosmic order rather than moral agents, but if they do punish sins such as lying or oath-breaking they do it in this life and not the next, in which there is generally little interest.

The world religions of the kind we are familiar with began developing in the Axial Age of the first millennium BC in the ancient literate civilisations at a time of growing urbanisation, commerce, warfare, and great social and intellectual turmoil in general. This generated a new class of thinkers and teachers who debated with one another about the meaning of life, how society should be organised, and the nature of the divine. Thinkers in these civilisations were searching for a more transcendent and universal authority on how one should live that went beyond the limits of their own society and traditions, and beyond the purely material prosperity and success that was the focus of tribal religion. "Everywhere one notices attempts to introduce greater purity, greater justice, greater perfection *and a more universal explanation of things*". They not only thought about society and the nature of Man in a new way, with a deeper awareness of the self and developing ideas of the soul. They were also developing the idea of Man as a thinking being, which gave him a unique status in the cosmos. Old images of the gods as crudely human were replaced by more transcendent and universal notions of the Divine as the source of cosmic order. The soul now came to be seen not as some crude vital essence but as the highest, sometimes the most intellectual part of the person, whose moral perfection is the route to salvation whereas the physical body is the source of hindrances to perfection—lust, gluttony, sloth, and greed, for example—because physical temptations are immediate and powerful obstacles to doing what is right, and powerful reinforcements of self-centredness. Denial of what we would call the ego through various forms of asceticism is therefore an essential element in all the world religions.

Since intellect and reason are uniquely human and set us apart from the animals, we have the very important idea that the essential and distinctive mental element in human beings, the soul, is akin to the creative and ordering element in the cosmos, of Man as microcosm in relation to the macrocosm. This profound doctrine takes us far beyond the crude formulation of the gods as beings who punish and reward human actions: it is a transition from Power to Wisdom, and is the real point of contact between the human and the divine in the transcendent systems of ethics that were formulated by the world religions. A major development in the reflections upon virtue is the marked growth in the spirit of love, of compassion and benevolence towards one's fellows, which is found in all the cultures of our study. Organised bodies of doctrine inspired by specific teachers developed during this period, and for the first time "religion" emerges as something distinct from society in the modern manner, which also created the possibility of new forms of social conflict. (On religious evolution see in particular Bellah 1970 and Barnes 2000.)

Even this briefest of summaries of the evolution of religion surely makes it clear that the notion of hypertrophy has absolutely nothing to contribute to our understanding of it. The development of theological doctrine, the growing awareness of the inner life of the individual, the notion of the immortal soul and its salvation, spiritual experience, the rejection of "the world, the flesh, and the devil", and the idea of the conversion of unbelievers are novel developments, constructed in the course of history, that can in no sense be traced back to the world of the hunter-gatherer, in however embryonic a form. I see no teeth of the baby elephant developing into tusks here, and instead we must fall back on the constructivist approach I have been advocating.

7. Mental modules

We can finally take up in more detail the theme of mental modules with which we began the chapter. According to Pinker and other evolutionary psychologists, "The mind is organised into modules or mental organs, each with a specialised design that makes it an expert in one arena of interaction with the world. The modules' basic logic is specified by our genetic program" (Pinker 1997:21). Each module is supposed to have been honed by natural selection as human beings adapted to the various problems of survival during our ancestors' long period of evolution in the Pleistocene epoch in East Africa, the Environment of Evolutionary Adaptation, or EEA. All organisms have basic biological needs, but the selectionist model also treats organisms as if they faced an environment filled with objective "problems", locks to which the right adaptive keys are selected from a series of random trials and errors. So for man, the use of fire for cooking food, the adoption of agriculture and the domestication of animals, the discovery of metals, and so on, were like a set of fixed obstacles in some assault course, which Man alone successfully overcame. Or, to change the metaphor, the environment is seen as composed of empty ecological "niches" waiting to be filled by organisms which become ever more exquisitely adapted to fit them by variation and selection. No one, of course, would deny that there are different sorts of environments—arctic tundra, tropical rain forests, underground caves with streams flowing through them, and so on—which offer different opportunities and constraints. But the concept of the ecological niche postulates a much more precise, adaptive fit between organism and environment than this. As Lewontin has pointed out:

> *To maintain that organisms adapt to the environment is to maintain that ... ecological niches exist in the absence of organisms and that evolution consists in filling these empty and pre-existent niches. But the external world can be divided up in a non-countable infinity of ways so that there is a non-countable infinity of conceivable ecological niches. Unless there is a preferred and correct way in which to partition the world, the idea of an ecological niche without an*

organism filling it loses all meaning. The alternative is that ecological niches are defined only by the organisms living in them *[my emphasis]…(Lewontin 1984:237–8).*

For example, we may imagine ancient hunter-gatherers close to a lake or river, in which it is clear that fish are swimming. While they *need* food of some kind, if they want to catch and eat the fish, then this is a *problem* which they or may not be able to solve. But if they believe that water is the boundary between their world and the spirit world, and that it would be dangerous to eat the fish, then catching them is not a problem. In other words problems don't have an independent existence in the real world like the rocks and tree stumps we can trip over: they are only problems in relation to human *purposes*, and once we accept this we have no reason to suppose that there is any need for modules in the first place. Instead, there is the imaginative exploration of the possibilities of the environment.

(a) The Universal Grammar module

The most famous example of a mental module is Chomsky's Universal Grammar. For Chomsky the basic or defining element of the language "organ" is recursion, recursion not simply in the sense of repeating the same process indefinitely, but where one clause is included or embedded in another: "The man is French" → "The man [whom you saw] is French" → The man [whom [[you said]] you saw] is French", and so on.

Recursion in this sense is the structure-building process par excellence, and I say that it is part of the language "organ" because Chomsky really believes that language is hard-wired into the physiology of the brain, and has a number of innate and universal characteristics:

All languages have a vocabulary in the thousands or tens of thousands, sorted into part-of-speech categories including noun and verb…. The higher levels of phrase structure include auxiliaries … which signify tense, modality, aspect, and negation. Nouns are marked for case and assigned semantic roles by the mental dictionary entry of the verb or other predicate. Phrases can be moved from their deep structure positions, leaving a gap or "trace", by a structure dependent movement rule, thereby forming questions, relative clauses, passives, and other widespread constructions. New word structures can be created and modified by derivational and inflectional rules. Inflectional rules primarily mark nouns for case and number, and mark verbs for tense, aspect, mood, voice, negation, and agreement with subjects and objects in number, gender, and person (Pinker 2015:235–6).

And some linguists make equally strong claims for the scope of a genetic basis of language:

Much remains to be done, but ... [e]ventually, the growth of language in a child will be viewed as similar to the growth of hair: just as hair emerges with a certain level of light, air, and protein, so, too, a biologically regulated language organ necessarily emerges under exposure to a random speech community (Anderson and Lightfoot 2000:21).

Chomsky maintains (2010:59) that the "language organ" resulted from a major genetic mutation, a rewiring of the brain in a single individual whom he names Prometheus, probably within the last 100,000 years, and linguists in the generative grammar tradition of Chomsky have therefore maintained that all languages must be equally complex (ALEC): "The innate cognitive machinery which is central to the generative concept of language competence is taken to be too comprehensive to leave room for significant differences with respect to complexity" (Sampson 2009:6–7).

When we actually look at languages spoken in primitive societies, however, we find that in many ways they are not nearly as complex as those spoken, and especially written, in modern developed societies. Recursion, which Chomsky claims is at the very heart of language, may be non-existent, or hardly present at all, and language in fact forms a spectrum from the simple to the complex that is related to the level of sociocultural complexity. Not all features of grammar, it is true, are developmentally significant, but there are a number of linguistic features that have strong developmental correlations. The first and most important of these concerns recursion itself, subordinate clauses or embedding, which is very weak or even absent in the simpler languages, and instead we find strings of short phrases simply strung together with very simple syntax. There is also a lack of relative pronouns; the repetitive use of conjunctions; no passive voice; no conditionals; a weak tense and mood system; no case markers; very limited use of prepositions; no comparatives or superlatives; no numbers; little in the way of logical quantifiers (some, all, each, every); or little or nothing in the way of intensional verbs—assume, want, think, believe—that might require embedding.

These features of the simple languages are typical of small homogeneous communities where strangers are relatively few, where all communication is face-to-face, where there is low division of labour, where technology is of a simple subsistence type, and where there is no literacy or schooling. In other words, where those speaking to each other are very familiar with the circumstances in which they are all concerned, so that utterances are heavily "context-dependent". On the other hand, the primary factors that remove context from communication and require more complex syntax are: where speakers and listeners are often strangers, from much larger groups, with a high division of labour and different life experiences, and in particular where writing is involved, which not only allows communication that is no longer face-to-face, as is necessarily the case with oral communication, but which also has properties of its own that favour grammatical complexity: "Without precise knowledge of the audience or immediate, simultaneous feedback from the audience … the writer is obliged to use words and syntax more accurately, deliberately, and elaborately. In conversation, the participants function as an immediate, concrete environment for one another" (Fondacaro & Higgins 1985:86). There is actually very good evidence that recursion, or "finite clause subordination" which is a prime example of a complex feature of language, has evolved in the course of history. For example:

Akkadian is one of the earliest languages to have been reduced to writing, and Deutscher claims that if one looks at the earliest recorded stages of Akkadian one finds a complete absence of [recursion]. What's more, this is not just a matter of the surviving records happening not to include examples of recursive structures that did exist in speech; Deutscher shows that if we inspect the 2,000-year history of Akkadian, we see [recursive] clauses gradually developing out of simpler, non-recursive structures which did exist in the early records. And Deutscher argues that this development was visibly a response to new communicative needs arising in Babylonian society (Sampson 2009:11).

The complex societies in which the written word becomes normal therefore develop a whole range of cultural subjects that require increasingly complex forms of thought: administrative documents, legislation, legal disputes and arguments, technical manuals for a variety of tasks, and more abstract interests such as the theory of government and philosophy, theology, and the natural sciences, all of which will require a more elaborate syntax. The idea of a language organ or module is clearly refuted by all this evidence (and see also Hallpike 2018b), and our only alternative is to propose a dialectical, constructive relationship between the properties of the human mind and the social relations between the individuals concerned. I therefore agree entirely that:

[G]rammar is the product of history (the processes that shape how languages are passed from one generation to the next) and human psychology (the set of social and cognitive capacities that allow generations to learn a language in the first place). More important, this theory proposes that language recruits brain systems that may not

*have evolved specifically for that purpose and so is a different idea to
Chomsky's single-gene mutation for recursion (Ibbotson & Tomasello
2016:74).*

(b) Mathematics and morality modules

Pinker claims (1997:338) that there is also a mathematics module, but
it is clear that there could not have been any selective pressure for such
a module to develop in the circumstances of the EEA. Even today
many simple cultures, especially hunter-gatherers but including some
shifting cultivators may only have words for single, pair, and many,
and we can get a good idea why this should be so from the example
of a Cree hunter from eastern Canada, who was asked in a court case
involving land how many rivers there were in his hunting territory,
and did not know:

> *The hunter knew every river in his territory individually and there-
> fore had no need to know how many there were. Indeed, he would
> know each stretch of each river as an individual thing and therefore
> had no need to know in numerical terms how long the rivers were.
> The point of the story is that we count things when we are ignorant
> of their individual identity—this can arise when we don't have
> enough experience of the objects, when there are too many of them
> to know individually, or when they are all the same, none of which
> conditions obtain very often for a hunter. If he has several knives
> they will be known individually by their different sizes, shapes, and
> specialised uses. If he has several pairs of moccasins they will be worn
> to different degrees, having been made at different times, and may
> be of different materials and design (Denny 1986:133).*

Again, the Tauade, like many peoples of Papua New Guinea, only
had words for single, *kone*, and pair, *kupariai*. While the Tauade engage in complex transactions of pork exchange they have never needed
to use a counting system to keep track of these because each exchange

is unique, between different persons, for different purposes and in different circumstances. Here too, like the Cree, *distinctive individual identity* is key to the lack of number and counting. (The Tauade had only recently adopted the Tok Pisin number system based on ten because they had to deal with modern money whose coins and notes have no individual identity.) So it was perfectly possible to survive without the need for verbal numerals or for counting, and consequently there could have been no selective pressure for arithmetical skills to evolve in the specific conditions of the EEA, and for any specific module to develop.

As we all know, mathematics has only flowered in the last few centuries, and among a tiny minority of people, far too brief a time-span for natural selection to have had the least effect. The mathematician Keith Devlin very reasonably concludes: "Whatever features of our brain enable (some of) us to do mathematics must have been present long before we had any mathematics. *Those crucial features, therefore, must have evolved to fulfil some other purpose*" [my emphasis] and are, as we shall see shortly, most properly described as "exaptations".

Again, Hauser in *Moral Minds* (2006) claims that we have an innate morality module, a "universal moral grammar", basically similar to Chomsky's generative grammar for language. Just as our innate generative grammar allows us to construct a limitless variety of correct sentences, so Hauser proposes that our universal moral grammar has "a capacity that enables each individual to unconsciously and automatically evaluate a limitless variety of actions in terms of principles that dictate what is permissible, obligatory, or forbidden" (ibid., 41). Moral thought, however, evolves in relation to social complexity, as we shall see in the next chapter, and this kind of development is incompatible with modularity. How, in any case, did natural selection manage to endow us with a module that could foresee the moral dilemmas we would face in complex industrial societies thousands of years before these had developed. In tribal societies, for example, members of the same kin group have very important moral obligations to help one another, but in modern states, for those in public office especially, this kind of behaviour is considered nepotistic, morally dubious at best, and possibly even criminal. I find it equally hard to imagine the Konso or the Tauade grappling with human rights, multiculturalism, nuclear weapons, or the ethical implications of veganism. How could any morality module, closely adapted to the hunter-gatherer bands of the Pleistocene, possibly deal with such dilemmas?

(c) The plausibility of modules

In more recent years, since evolutionary psychologists first began advancing the notion that our minds evolved specialised cognitive modules during the EEA, our knowledge of how the brain works has increased exponentially, and the whole idea of mental modules is now distinctly *passé*. For example "…there are many different system organisations that can produce the same kind of behaviour a strictly modular system does and … they may not be distinguishable from it by any conceivable experimental strategy….Nonlinear, interconnected, dynamic systems [such as the brain] are fully capable of producing the kind of behaviour expected from modular systems" (Uttal 2001:182–3).

Indeed, culture itself can modify the way in which the brain operates:

> *Neuroplastic research has shown us that every sustained activity ever mapped—including physical activities, sensory activities, learning, thinking, and imagining—changes the brain as well as the mind. Cultural ideas and activities are no exception. Our brains are modified by the cultural activities we do—be they reading, studying music, or learning new languages. We all have what might be called a culturally modified brain, and as cultures evolve, they continually lead to new changes in the brain (Doidge 2007:288).*

While there is undoubtedly some cognitive specialisation in the brain, as in the different functions of the two hemispheres (see McGilchrist 2012), there must be a limit to this:

It would simply not be feasible to construct a brain that allocates a specific psychological module to every conceivable event an individual might encounter, as the costs in terms of neural circuitry and information processing would be huge. There is no intrinsic virtue to mental specificity: general solutions will be favoured when they can do a good enough job at low cost.... Domain general processes are no more incompatible with evolutionary theory than domain-specific processes (Laland and Brown 2002:182–3).

Tooby and Cosmides, Pinker, and other sociobiologists habitually talk about adaptation as successful problem-solving, which has then been incorporated in the various modules, but their notion of modules still does not come close to answering Wallace's objection that natural selection can only operate in relation to current conditions, not those that might exist thousands of years later. How, then, could there be a Stone-Age mathematics module that can deal with calculus, or a morality module that can deal with problems of human rights? Like so many extreme Darwinists, they have been led far astray by their obsession with adaptation, as Stephen J. Gould explains very convincingly by the concept of "exaptation". An exaptation is some characteristic that was either selected for some other function, or not originally selected for anything, but in changed conditions can work in new and different ways that do have survival value, and the example he gives is the brain:

A. R. Wallace, a strict adaptationist if ever there was one, nonetheless denied that natural selection had built the human brain. "Savages" (living primitives), he argued, have mental equipment equal to ours, but maintain only a rude and primitive culture—that is, they do not use most of their mental capacities and natural selection can only build for immediate use. Darwin, who was not a strict adaptationist, was both bemused and angered. He recognised the hidden fallacy in Wallace's argument: that the brain, though undoubtedly built by selection for some complex set of functions, can, as a result of its intricate structure, work in an unlimited number of ways quite unrelated to the selective pressure that constructed it [my emphasis]. Many of these ways might become important, if not indispensable, for future survival in later social contexts.... But current utility carries no automatic implication about historical origin. Most of what the brain now does to enhance our survival lies in the domain of exaptation—and does not allow us to make hypotheses about the selective paths of human history. How much of the evolutionary literature on human behavior would collapse if we incorporated the principle of exaptation into the core of our evolutionary thinking? This collapse would be constructive because it would vastly broaden our range of hypotheses, and focus attention on current function and development (all testable propositions) instead of leading us to unprovable reveries about primal fratricide on the African savanna or dispatching mammoths at the edge of great ice sheets—a valid subject, but one better treated in novels... (Gould & Vrba 1982:14).

8. Conclusions

Sociobiologists such as Tooby and Cosmides, and E. O. Wilson are prominent advocates for the unification of all science, in which they include the social sciences and the humanities. So Wilson says that in his youth, after reading Ernst Mayr on the neo-Darwinian synthesis, he suddenly saw the world in a wholly new way:

I had experienced the Ionian Enchantment. That recently coined expression I borrow from the physicist and historian Gerald Holton. It means a belief in the unity of the sciences—a conviction far deeper than a mere working proposition, that the world is orderly and can be explained by a small number of natural laws [my emphasis].

Its roots go back to Thales of Miletus, in Ionia, in the sixth century BC.... But the spell of the Enchantment extends to other fields of science as well [as physics], and in the minds of a few it reaches beyond into the social sciences, and still further ... to touch the humanities (Wilson 1998:4–5).

"The spell of the Enchantment" puts its finger rather more perceptively than Wilson might have wished on the somewhat fanatical, True Believer qualities of the Universal Darwinists and the sociobiologists I have been criticising, and gives us an important insight into their state of mind and their craving for simplicity. To what extent the idea of the unity of the sciences and the humanities is justifiable is a profound question which I leave to another occasion, but what can be said with absolute certainty is that it will not be going anywhere until its advocates are prepared to master the facts, which in my case are those of anthropology. In the course of this book, however, we have encountered again and again what can fairly be described as a reckless indifference to the facts. Yet another example of this is E. O. Wilson's theory that homosexuals could have increased their inclusive fitness in primitive societies by assisting their close relatives in child care, which is why homosexual genes have survived in the human genome instead of being selected out as one might expect:

The homosexual members of primitive societies could have helped members of the same sex, either while hunting and gathering or in more domestic occupations at the dwelling sites. Free from the special obligations of parental duties, they would have been in a position to operate with special efficiency in assisting close relatives. They might further have taken the roles of seers, shamans, artists, and keepers of tribal knowledge. If the relatives—sisters, brothers, nieces, nephews, and others—were benefited by higher survival and reproductive rates [my emphasis], the genes these individuals shared with the homosexual specialists would have increased at the expense of alternative genes. Inevitably, some of these genes would have been those that predisposed individuals toward homosexuality (Wilson 2004:145).

The existence of homosexual genes is a matter of some doubt, but Wilson's hypothesis of the helpful, nepotistic gay uncles and aunties increasing their inclusive fitness by looking after their nieces and nephews is not to my knowledge (Hallpike 2018:33–6) supported by any ethnographic evidence whatsoever, and his ideas are in fact completely uninformed speculation. His theory in any case is based on a simple fallacy: he assumes, quite wrongly, that homosexuals can't (or won't) have children, whereas there is plenty of evidence from anthropology, the classical world, and more recent history, that homosexuals of both genders are quite capable, in most cases, of marrying and begetting children. Given the enormous social pressure for marriage in traditional societies, notably among hunter-gatherers, it is far simpler than Wilson's scenario, and more in accordance with the known facts, merely to assume that if these genes for homosexuality exist, they were perpetuated by those with homosexual inclinations who nevertheless married and begot children, thereby making their "homosexual" genes invisible to natural selection.

Notes

1. Not, however, E. O. Wilson, who was a keen advocate of the meme (originally as the "culturgen" in Lumsden & Wilson 1981) which he regarded as the basic unit of culture and "the node of semantic memory and its correlate in brain activity" (Wilson 1998:148).

Chapter IV
Developmental psychology and cultural evolution

The central place of human selection in cultural evolution means that understanding not just human nature but also how people think and learn must be of the first importance. There is in fact a vast body of evidence from anthropology and psychology that the members of non-literate, small-scale primitive societies with simple technologies do not in many ways think like the educated members either of ancient civilisations or of modern industrial societies. Modern scientific thought, indeed, has only developed in the last few hundred years, just as philosophy only developed with the literate civilisations of antiquity. Many Victorians believed that the brains of people whose societies had developed relatively little science and technology, such as those in Australia, Melanesia, or Africa, were therefore different from those of other peoples, such as the Chinese, Indians, and Europeans, where these had become highly developed. But we now know that this was mistaken because African or Melanesian children from non-literate, tribal societies can, if sent to Western types of schools and universities, learn modern science.

If human cognitive abilities have not remained the same over the last ten thousand years since the adoption of agriculture, but have evolved through interaction with the rest of culture and social organisation, this introduces a very significant new factor into our understanding of cultural evolution. If the kinds of thinking embodied in this book, for example, were not available to members of pre-literate societies, this must have had very important consequences for the ways in which they could think about their society, their technology, and the natural world. In the same way, if abstract, philosophical thought first became available to the educated elite of the ancient civilisations, this too must have had very powerful consequences for the kinds of society and belief systems that developed, as we saw when discussing the evolution of religion. The way in which the mind develops by interaction with the social and physical environment is the subject-matter of developmental psychology, but there is no way, however, that sociobiologists, with their pre-programmed cognitive modules, can take on board the idea of significant cognitive development as a result of social interaction and experience. This is why, for example, Chomsky and his followers claim that all languages must be equally complex. Anthropologists, too, from a very different point of view, have always been dogmatically opposed to the use of psychology to explain cultural phenomena, and we need to understand the reason for this before we consider developmental psychology.

1. Psychology and "collective representations"

When anthropologists talk about the "thought" of primitive peoples they are referring in particular to systems of classification, time-reckoning, number, causal explanations of events, notions of space, grammar, myths, magic, and belief systems. These are commonly referred to as "collective representations" because they are cultural patterns of thought that have been acquired by individuals in the course of their upbringing. This notion of collective representations is entirely reasonable, but in the very influential Durkheimian tradition collective representations are *purely* social in origin, and are then supposed to be passively absorbed by individuals in their upbringing. For example, Durkheim explains the origins of the categories of space, time, logical class, and causality as the product of social organisation:

World space has been primitively constructed on the model of social space, that is to say of the territory occupied by the society and such that the society represents to itself; time expresses the rhythm of collective life; the idea of kind [logical class] was originally nothing else than another aspect of the idea of a human group; the collective power [of the group] and its impact on consciousness served as prototypes for the notion of force and of causality (Durkheim 1913:36).

The anthropologist Max Gluckman gives a perfect illustration of Durkheimian thinking:

Perceptions, emotions, evaluations of right and wrong, ideas of the causes of events—in short, whole systems of thought and feeling … exist transcendentally, independently of the individuals in whom they appear. They are what the French sociologists call collective representations, *which pass from generation to generation, learnt in behaviour, continued in proverb and precept, in the technology and conventions and ritual, and, with the development of writing, in books. A man's psyche is social, not organic (Gluckman 1949:75).*

The dogma that "a man's psyche is social, not organic" is another classic example of linear causal thinking: social organisation produces collective representations, which then mould the minds of all the individual members of the society, just as the genotype "moulds" the body. The process of learning is assumed to be nothing more than the passive copying by children of what adults do and say, the bit-by-bit accumulation of knowledge like an empty bucket being slowly filled. As societies develop greater complexity, by such processes as the increasing division of labour, collective representations also become more complex, but the Durkheimians are sure that the individual is essentially passive in this whole process and can only receive what has been transmitted. But one only has to reflect on the history of one's own culture to realise the absurd exaggeration of the whole Durkheimian model.

The Darwinian theory of evolution and human origins, for example, has certainly become a collective representation of modern Western society that replaced an earlier representation based on the biblical creation story of Adam and Eve in the Garden of Eden. But we know in detail about the thought processes by which Darwin and others developed their theory of evolution. Millions of students now absorb this theory in their biology lessons without personally having to go through all the steps that Darwin did, and some students will understand the theory much better than others. To this extent the collective representation "Darwinian evolution" transcends the minds of particular individuals, but the minds of individuals nevertheless played an essential part in the development and transmission of evolutionary theory. It should be fairly obvious, then, that collective representations both mould, and are moulded by, the thought of individuals in a complex interactive process.

In addition, the collective representations of complex societies will also be cognitively more powerful in certain respects than those of simple societies, but this question too has been thoroughly confused by orthodox modern anthropological thought on the subject. The following is a typical example:

> *I for one consider it unthinkable to claim that a Piaroa of the Venezuelan rain forest is irrational when he says that rain is the urine of the deity Ofo Da'a. The Westerner asserting that rain is H_2O and the Piaroa saying that it is the urine of a deity are doing so on similar grounds; both are relying on the knowledge of the supreme authority of their society, respectively the scientist and the shaman, on the nature of water (Overing 1985:4–5).*

But Overing evades two essential issues. One is that it is cognitively much *easier* to understand the Piaroa notion of rain than the Western version. It is no doubt true that in meteorological matters many of us are in the same state of dependency on our scientists as the Piaroa are on their shamans. To think of clouds dropping rain as like spraying

one's garden with a hose, as some of us do, is indeed no more cognitively demanding than thinking of it as the urine of a deity. But those
of us whose grasp of the nature of rainfall is restricted to this level are
not really participating in Western scientific culture at all in so far as
it deals with meteorology.

To think of rainfall scientifically, as an example of condensation, we
have to understand the idea of a given *volume* of air and of the total
mass of the water evaporated in that volume of air. This in turn gives
us the *density* of the water vapour and we then have to understand
that for a given volume of air there is a maximum density of water
vapour that can be absorbed, at which point the air is *saturated*, that
is, its *relative humidity* is 100%, otherwise known as the dew point.
(But saturation also depends upon the pressure of the air and its
temperature.) When cooled further the airborne water vapour will
condense to form liquid water, that is, rain. The condensation of
water vapour into rain is therefore associated with changes in the linked
parameters of air volume, temperature, pressure, and humidity. This
very brief sketch of only a small part of the scientific theory of rainfall
shows quite clearly that understanding science is not simply a matter
of accepting authority but also of grasping a set of conceptual relations
between variables, of percentages and ratios (both direct and inverse),
of distinguishing between volume and mass, and of understanding
the reciprocal relations between a number of related variables in a
total system. The ideas of mass, volume, density, inverse proportion
and so on are indeed cultural conventions, but they are nevertheless
conventions that are inherently more difficult to understand than the
convention that rainfall is the urine of a deity. The Piaroa belief that
this is the origin of rain, and the Konso belief that rain comes from
the Sky God, and falls on the just but not on the unjust, are complete
in themselves. They rest on no further elaborate theory of how exactly
the Sky God's moral judgements are transformed into water droplets,
or of how Ofo Da'a urinates, and they are as beliefs extremely simple
and can be understood by children.

Secondly, Overing evades the problem that some cultures' beliefs are more adequate accounts of the world than others'—the fact that rainfall is not, in reality, the urine of a deity at all but the condensation of water vapour. How, then, did our scientists reach a more adequate understanding of this phenomenon than the Piaroa and other primitive peoples? To say that those concepts on which the scientific theory of rainfall such as mass, volume, density, saturation, and so on are cultural conventions accepted on authority, and so might easily have been different, is clearly inadequate. They were developed out of the experience and thinking of individuals in the solution of real problems, without whose intellectual efforts our more adequate forms of knowledge could not have developed. To be sure, these individuals could not have thought as they did without an existing body of collective representations which they could use as a basis for thinking about nature or society, but they in turn enriched and developed the collective representations of their culture so that they provided the foundations for new developments. Unless we recognise that collective representations are also the expression of individual thought and experience we have no means of explaining how organised systems of knowledge about the real world can have developed at all. Once, however, it is accepted that the thinking of individuals must be an integral part of the generation and transmission of collective representations, we then have to ask how those individuals learn.

The idea that we have acquired new cognitive skills in the course of cultural evolution throws an entirely fresh light on the old problem of primitive thought, because to understand how new cognitive skills develop we can study living people, rather than speculating endlessly about our unknowable ancestors in the Pleistocene. We can actually learn a great deal about how culture has evolved from the studies of how the thinking of children develops that have been made by developmental psychologists, such as Piaget, in very extensive studies of children from all round the world. The reason is simple: the child finds some ideas and ways of thinking much easier than others, whether we are talking of the natural or the social worlds, but the child will only master the more difficult forms of thought if he has to face situations that involve them in daily life, and also if his culture can provide the intellectual tools for solving them, such as writing, books and schooling. If these conditions are lacking, then in some respects the thinking of adults will not develop significantly beyond that of children, but these forms of thought will still be quite adequate for people to get by in ordinary life, an excellent case of the survival of the mediocre. So, the next question is how people actually learn.

2. Developmental psychology

For much of the twentieth century the most influential theory of learning was B. F. Skinner's Behaviourism, which was essentially Darwinian. The essence of Behaviourism is "operant conditioning": the organism emits a behaviour, an operant, initially in a random way like a mutation, and this is either positively or negatively reinforced or conditioned by the environment, causing it to be retained or discarded from the behavioural repertoire. Skinner himself explicitly regarded his theory of learning as Darwinian: "As accidental traits, arising from mutations, are selected by their contribution to survival, so accidental variations in behaviour are selected by their reinforcing consequences" (Skinner 1974:114), and in both theories the organism is essentially passive in relation to the environment. According to Skinner, the environment shapes us in two fundamental ways—through our biological inheritance by natural selection, and through the positive and negative reinforcement our behaviour receives from other people and the physical world. "A person does not act on the world, the world acts upon him" (1971:21). Behaviourism, however, has been thoroughly discredited, particularly by Chomsky, who pointed out that children, for example, acquire grammatically correct language without ever having previously heard many of the sentences they produce.

The traditional anthropologists' model of learning as passive copying of adult models, or the Dawkins model of memes parasitizing our brains, the Skinnerian model of operant conditioning, and the sociobiologists' modules are all failures, based on linear causal models, in which the individual is always passive, and we need to turn to developmental psychology instead, specifically to the work of Piaget. Developmental psychology, as formulated by Piaget (and which he called "genetic epistemology", "the genesis of knowledge")[1] takes the diametrically opposite view that the individual is an *agent*, acting upon the world in order to understand it. The whole thrust of the argument from developmental psychology is that there are no inherited mental modules, but that individual thinking develops as an interaction between the knower and the known.

Piaget rejected the whole idea of learning as the passive absorption of knowledge, and regarded the individual as actively exploring his environment from birth onwards. Cognitive growth is an aspect of general organic adaptation to the environment, in which process neither the hereditary characteristics of the organism nor the structure of the environment are sufficient to explain the patterns of growth of the organism. Thought is a self-regulating system which tries to achieve equilibrium with its environment by constructing *stable* representations that transcend the variability and fluctuations of experience. Cognitive development, therefore, cannot simply be the product of biological maturation but proceeds through a series of stages that involve the successive *reorganisation* of thought around action, imagery, and verbal representation. It is important to realise that these stages are not rigidly bounded but on the contrary change gradually from one to the next. They are age-related, but their chronology also depends on the social milieu, which can have a stimulating or retarding effect, and even prevent further cognitive growth beyond a certain stage (Piaget 1977:815).

Since Piaget believed that cognitive growth was the result of an interaction between the individual and the cultural milieu, he therefore rejected both the Durkheimian model of collective representations as determining individual thought as well as the opposite view, typical of sociobiology, that they are simply the genetically programmed outcome of individual thought processes (Piaget 1971:114). His theory of the development of knowledge in the individual is therefore a transformational, interactive theory of the same general type as my constructivist theory of cultural evolution.

The human mind is not then like an empty bucket that is gradually filled with information by adults, or by passively observing the world around one; each individual has *actively* to construct his understanding of the world, of things and of people, by interacting and experimenting with it himself. While we are born into a particular culture, which we did not make, our culture can only be transmitted by individuals, including ourselves, so what the majority of individuals can understand must have a fundamental effect on the kinds of ideas and beliefs that can develop over time in any culture.

Some ways of thinking are more elementary than others, and provide the foundation on which the more advanced and complex types of thought can be constructed, when the social conditions are right. But, as we shall see, it is quite possible for simple modes of thought to survive perfectly well in simple societies. We can begin by looking at how children's knowledge of the physical world develops. They do not learn merely by copying adults but by *their own activity and experiments* on the objects around them, and by assimilating the results of these into their own modes of thought. For example, infants below about 18 months (who are at what is called the sensori-motor stage of mental development) have to construct a stable view of the world around them entirely without the assistance of adults; they have to learn that toys do not really vanish when they are hidden behind a cushion but continue to exist and can be found again; that objects do not really get bigger when they get closer, and smaller when they get farther away; and they have to learn how to co-ordinate what they see with what they hear and with what they can touch. They achieve this understanding of the physical world by actions, not by words, and by patterns of actions that are repeated with an increasing range of objects, and with increasing discrimination as they learn what different objects are good for. They also come to realise that they, too, are objects in a stable world of other permanent objects, and this general process of development is the same for all infants whether they grow up in a hunter-gatherer society or in a modern city.

At about 18 months they start to form mental images of different aspects of the world. These images are not just visual but involve imitating the actions and events that the child is trying to understand, and he can communicate these images to other people not only by imitation but, increasingly, by language and also, if the means are available, by drawing and models. This is the beginning of what is often called the "pre-operational" stage of thought, which in its later years, roughly 4–7, is known as "intuitive" thought. It is during this stage that, intellectually, the child starts to break out of its private world and to become a social being who can participate in culture. From this point on, the child's society and general environment start to have a major influence on his intellectual development. Imagery allows the child to perform actions internally in its own mind, and is therefore a major advance on pure physical activity. But the fact that the child can now represent the world to himself in imagery, and refer to it in words, means that while it is possible for him to think that he understands what is happening, in fact there are major problems that prevent these image-based representations from corresponding with reality in some respects.

So, for example, if a child of three or four is asked to draw the stages by which a curved piece of wire or stick is straightened he will do it something like this:

This is obviously wrong, because in reality the ends would get farther apart, but children at this stage are unable to analyse processes and co-ordinate their different elements, such as the relations between the curvature of the wire and the distance between the ends. They tend to concentrate, to "centre" their minds, on *one* aspect or dimension of the event and ignore the others, and are generally unable to hold two related but different ideas in the mind at once. If a child at the intuitive stage is asked, for example, to arrange a series of ten blocks in order of size he will be unable to do so: while he can say that this one is bigger than that one, he cannot grasp that the same block may be *both* bigger than one and smaller than another. Without understanding this, it is impossible to construct a series of blocks from smallest to largest.

Again, if these children are shown water being poured from a short, fat glass into a tall, thin glass they will say that there is more water in the tall thin glass because they are concentrating on one dimension alone, the height, and not taking the different diameters of the two glasses into account as well. They cannot "conserve" quantity—realise that it remains the same—because they cannot operate with two different dimensions simultaneously, and understand that an increase in one is *compensated* by an equal decrease in the other. While the child may agree that if the water were poured back into the short fat glass there would be the same quantity as before, he still believes that there is more water in the tall thin glass. It is as if pouring back the water from the second glass into the first were completely unrelated to pouring from the first glass into the second, and without understanding re-versibility, process presents major problems. Compensation between height and diameter has first to be grasped before the pouring back, the *reversibility*, can be understood as a crucial test that something—in this case quantity—has remained the same, or been conserved, despite the changes in appearance.

Whereas intuitive thought remains tied to the *appearance* of things, to static and *unco-ordinated imagery*, development beyond this involves "concrete-operational" thinking, building up systems of thought that can cope with transformations in the appearances of things, and realise how some properties remain the same throughout these transformations. Conservation, based on *compensation* and *reversibility*, is an essential element of these stable systems of relations; but operations also involve *decentration*, the ability to think of things as having more than one relation at a time—like the block that is both bigger than one and smaller than another. Operational, unlike intuitive thinking, is therefore a much more powerful means of understanding the world; it is "systems thinking", in which the parts and the whole can be thought about together, in mobile and dynamic relationships, without the contradictions inherent in static, *image-based* thought.

In our society the ability to conserve quantity typically starts developing around the age of six, but the conservation of other properties such as length, weight, area and volume takes several more years, and the same is true of an operational grasp of number, space, time, and classification, about which I shall say more in a moment. Concrete operational thinking is therefore bound up with the sorts of practical problems in weighing and measuring that we encounter in daily life on, say, a construction site, or when we are doing some DIY in our home. It also involves a basic mechanical understanding of how things work, of how the pedals on our bicycle drive the wheels, for example, and so we would expect it to be developed by experience of technology, in particular.

The development of what is called "formal operational" thought goes beyond concrete thinking, and begins to occur in our sort of society during adolescence, if children have the appropriate schooling and the opportunity to experiment, and is basic to scientific and philosophical thinking. Whereas concrete-operational thought is limited to thinking about relations between actual objects and events, the formal operational thinker can consider systems of relations in a much more abstract way, without the need for concrete examples. He also begins to understand thinking about thinking and the role of the mind in understanding the world, and the logical implications of statements;

he can consider hypothetical situations in the form of statements about them, and so can mentally review all the possible (as distinct from the actual) combinations of factors and variables that could be involved. This allows the person to understand probability, to produce experimental hypotheses and work out methods of testing them, to be able to carry out purely logical deductions based on verbal statements alone, and to think about his society as a whole and to speculate about ideal political arrangements. I must emphasise, however, that not only do people not leap from one stage of intellectual development to the next, but that they are often at different stages in relation to different sorts of problem, depending on the circumstances in which they have grown up. Even in our own type of modern society, not more than about 50% even of adults are capable of formal operational thought, and there will also be many people whose thinking is at the formal level, for example, in the understanding of political and ethical issues, but still at the level of concrete operations in mechanical problems.

This development from intuitive to formal operational thinking also involves profound changes in two other major areas of our relations with the physical world. One is in our awareness of our own thoughts and feelings, and the other is the distinction between the social and natural worlds, but I shall deal with these later. I first want to focus on the obvious parallel between the intuitive or pre-operational thinking that psychologists have described among children, and the type of thinking so often described by anthropologists in primitive society.

3. Developmental psychology and primitive thought

It is not really very surprising that even adult members of technologically primitive societies should have the same difficulties as children of six or seven in our society in solving problems of area and volume, or the relations between speed, time and distance, simply because they have never had to puzzle themselves about such things. In the same way, language is only experienced as speech, bound up in practical situations and dialogue between real people, rather than as something encountered in writing that can be analysed on the page. This means that there is a vast range of problems that can never even occur to the members of primitive society, but which our children will encounter in their daily lives and at school. Our children are also provided with the means to solve these problems by their schooling, and the resources of their culture generally, which are completely lacking in primitive society.

One of the most firmly established conclusions of cross-cultural developmental psychology is that formal operational thought is not found at all in primitive, pre-literate, small-scale societies. Indeed, for the most part the members of these societies can get by with very little in the way of concrete operational thought as well (Hallpike 1979). The prevalence of pre-operational, intuitive, thinking in primitive society is very much an example of the survival of the mediocre. We can now look in more detail at some parallels between intuitive notions of number, space, time, and classification and those found in hunter-gatherer and tribal societies.

A good example to begin is this problem about a house in a garden. In the first picture, A, there is a garden with a house in the middle, while in B the house is in the corner of the garden:

We are capable of concrete-operational thought, and realise that the amount of ground in the garden stays the same (is conserved), because we can think in terms of area as the product of length times breadth. Then it is obvious that the area of the garden minus that of the house has to be the same in both cases. But the normal response, whether of adults or children, at the intuitive stage, is to say that there is more ground in B, because their thinking is dominated by imagery, and the garden in B looks bigger.

When tests of conservation have been given to adolescents and adults in non-literate, tribal societies it has been found that a high percentage of them cannot conserve area, or quantity, or volume either. They are nevertheless perfectly capable of getting through the day without this ability because they live in what, technologically, is a very simple world in which they do not need to think about area or to pour water from short fat glasses into tall thin ones. But it is not just a matter of the lack of jugs and glasses in primitive society. There is also a general lack of measurement, with no standard units, no rulers, no scales and weights, and no clocks or other ways of measuring time apart from looking at the position of the sun. The lack of measurement means that it is very difficult to think about things in terms of their different dimensions. So while there are always words for big and small, heavy and light, long and short, or near and far, there are no words for size, weight, length, or distance, while big and small, or heavy and light, are seen as different and opposite, not as different points on the same scale or dimension.

Since dimensional thinking and measurement scarcely occur at all in primitive society, this means that ideas of number also remain very undeveloped. Here we need to remember the emphasis in primitive cultures on the *individuality* of things as opposed to their general qualities, like money, where one ten-dollar bill is identical with all others. If any counting occasionally needs to be done, they can use fingers (and toes), or stones, or notches in sticks or bones, or knots in a piece of string, to record the totals of things, without any words for numbers at all, and where number words exist they are often no higher than two or three. This relative lack of number words is found throughout Australia, much of Papua New Guinea, the Bushmen of the Kalahari, and some of the hunter-gatherers of South America. It is a good illustration that something we regard as absolutely necessary, and unthinkable to be without, has really had rather a short history in human culture, and that people with very simple technologies can get along quite well without counting in words.

Not surprisingly, when systems of number words develop they are almost always based on the five, ten, or twenty suggested by the fingers and toes, with decimal systems being by far the commonest. But the early use of numbers is thoroughly concrete, bound to the physical objects that are counted. When the Kpelle of Liberia, for example, put objects together, take them away, or share them among sets of people, they never work with pure numbers but always with objects as well—"2 chickens and 3 chickens make 5 chickens", but the expression "2 and 3 are 5" would not be understood (Gay & Cole 1967). In Papua New Guinea, "Systems of counting seem to be used entirely for counting numbers of concrete objects, such as wives, children, houses, pigs, and in the case of the larger counting systems [such as "round the body" systems] the numbers of shells to make a bride price" (Prince 1969:31).

Primitive counting, then, does not treat numbers as abstract classes that are arranged in a series from smaller to greater, but simply as groups of concrete objects each with a rigid and static association with a finger or other body part, or a name. It is only when people in the ancient civilisations started having to *measure* things, such as length, area, volume, weight, and so on and then do *calculations* with these figures, such as the number of mud-bricks needed for a wall of a certain size, that they could develop a more advanced understanding of number. Think, for example, of the tiresome calculations we have to make when we are ordering wall-paper for a room, when we have to work out the area of the walls, minus the openings, and then relate this to the width and length of the rolls of paper to calculate how many rolls we want. To do this we need to understand how addition, subtraction, multiplication, and division are related, so that we can see, for example, that 4 x 3 is carried out by 3 successive additions of a group of 4, and produces the same result as 4 successive additions of a group of 3, and that division, in the same way, is a sequence of subtractions. The result is that people will be able to grasp numbers in an operational way as mobile *hierarchies* of classes, instead of static collections of objects. For example, 12 can be seen as composed of 3 groups of 4, or 4 groups of 3, 6 groups of 2, or 2 groups of 6, and so on. They will also be able to understand the relation between cardinal numbers, which express quantity, and ordinal numbers, which express order, so that the cardinal number 4 also occupies the 2nd position in the series 1, 4, 8…

We have seen that in primitive society area is not thought of as length times breadth, and space in general is not thought of in terms of the straight lines, dimensions, and angles that we take for granted, but intuitively in terms of what is known as "topological" space. This takes no account of angles, or straight lines, or distances, or co-ordinates, and is often compared to a rubber sheet. If, say, a face is drawn on this sheet, however it is pulled, stretched, and distorted, all the basic features of eyes, nose, mouth, and ears will all stay in the same relative positions to each other, however much the angles and distances between them may change. Topologically, the eyes are each *separated* from the nose but are *next* to it; they are in a certain *order*—eye/nose/eye—so the nose is between or *included* by the two eyes. If we think about a landscape in a similar way it is easy to see that its various features can be thought about as those of separation, "next-to" or proximity, order, and between-ness or inclusion, and in a primitive environment understanding these will be enough to represent the physical world.

Village layouts and sacred places with their centre, boundary, and gates are like faces. Because topological space is closely related to actual physical features it easily acquires symbolic values. In one New Guinea tribe, for example, the coconut represents the centre of the hamlet, the areca palm the boundary, and the sago palm the bush. Again, the East is very widely associated with the rising sun and is therefore life-giving and auspicious, and people may be buried facing that direction when they die, whereas the West is bad because it is associated with the setting sun and with death. The body and the house are the focus of basic topological concepts like right and left, high and low, centre/periphery/and outside.

So topological space is essentially *static*, concrete and image-based, unlike our geometrical and projective space, which is designed to deal with every possible *movement* and *transformation* of position and shape, and is the same everywhere. Among the Temne of Africa, for example, the cardinal points are not used to co-ordinate movement and position in space, but have a static, symbolic meaning, such as east representing birth, and west representing death. "For us the cardinal points are co-ordinates for establishing location. The Temne never use them in this way, though should the necessity arise they will use one of them to indicate the general direction in which a place lies. Their cardinal points contain [symbolic] meanings which qualify activities and events in various ways" (Littlejohn 1963:9).

Topological space is therefore quite inadequate when we want to represent actual tracks, positions, and bearings of different locations on some kind of map, or even to measure the area of a piece of land, as we saw in the problem about the two gardens. An operational, geometrical understanding of space, based on dimensions and measurements, only develops, however, where land has to be measured with some exactness, as in the ancient civilisations, or where long-distance navigation becomes highly specialised, as in Polynesia.

The intuitive understanding of time also has severe limitations. Everyone, including little children, can understand process as a succession of events, because our whole lives consist of processes of one sort or another, from getting up in the morning to going to sleep at night, the rising and setting of the sun, the course of the seasons, the growth of plants and animals, and so on. In primitive society, like our own, the day will often be divided into conventional periods, such as "breakfast", "taking out the cattle to graze", "noon", and so on. There may be weeks made up of market days, and a sequence of named months in which different agricultural activities are carried out, the whole of which form a year. So calendars treat events as if they were points or stretches along a path; just as in topological space all we need to know to find point G, for example, is where it is located in the sequence E, F, G, H, I, so in "topological" time all we need to know is where "bringing the cattle home" comes in relation to "midday meal" and "dusk". In this sense, intuitive time is a kind of static, spatialized time like the static features of a landscape, and in the same way as places in a landscape, some events are more distant from another in time than others. In intuitive time, then, one only needs to know the order in which things come (succession), and whether they last a relatively long or a short time (duration).

The Tauade had no words for week, month, or year, and yet they had a word that can be translated as "time", *lova*: *oilova*, "this time", "now"; *telova*? "What time, when?"; *opolovan*, "olden time". But what they really mean by *lova* is merely "sequence of events". So *oilova* would more accurately be translated as "this sequence of events", i.e. the sequence of events in which the speakers are presently involved in; and *telova* "will you go to Port Moresby?", "in what sequence of events will you go to Port Moresby?", "after the plane has brought my letters to the mission". But sequences of standard events do not form measurable series like the hours of a 24-hour clock: one cannot say that three twilights equal one morning, or that from first light to going out into the fields is the same amount of time as from the coming back of the cattle until supper time.[2]

While people realise that some periods of time last longer than others—walking to a near village as opposed to a distant one, for example—we do not find that the journeys of the two walkers are ever directly compared, as in a race. This means that the relations between speed, time, and distance are never explored in intuitive thought, whereas operational time depends on a grasp of the relations between them. In primitive society the relative speeds of moving people or objects are not important issues in daily life, and in any case there are normally no means of measuring either time or distance. But let us suppose, for example, that two cars, 1 and 2, start from two points A_1 and A_2 simultaneously, and travel on two parallel tracks towards B_1 and B_2 and then stop at the same instant:

1 A_1..B_1
2 A_2...B_2

To understand this problem involves, first of all, a grasp of simultaneity: of course, we can all see if two things happen together, if it starts to rain just as we set off on a walk, or if the sun is setting when we come home, but the simultaneity of operational time involves two processes and judging when they both start *and stop* in relation to each other, which is essential for understanding the relation between time, speed, and distance. If car 1 goes faster than car 2 it will travel farther than 2 in a given period of time, but someone who is still at the intuitive level in the understanding of time will think that they could not have stopped simultaneously. This is because to such a person the car that travels the longer distance must have taken a longer time to do so, while travelling a shorter distance must take less time, and they think this because they cannot take account of the different speeds of the two cars, and understand how greater speed will cover a greater distance *in the same time*. A concrete operational grasp of time understands that the amount of time taken for the journey has to be calculated by dividing the distance covered by the speed at which someone travels. Without grasping this, the notion of time is therefore tied to distance and remains spatialized. This elementary relationship between speed, time, and distance is a good example of operational thinking, because someone who understands it will also realise that distance covered is the product of the speed and the time, and that speed is the distance divided by the time—a mobile system of transformations.

So we find that in the myths and stories of primitive and even traditional societies there are never accounts of two sequences of events going on simultaneously and being correlated by the narrator: "The king called all his nobles to a great feast to celebrate his victory, but *meanwhile* in the countryside the peasants were plotting their rebellion". There are no "meanwhiles" in folk tales.

Classification is an absolutely basic mental function, but some sorts of classification are easier than others. We can classify taxonomically, in terms of logical classes, but pre-operational classification tends to make use of what is called "functional entailment", which focuses on how things are related in ordinary life. So the question "What do dogs and rabbits have in common?" is answered taxonomically by saying that they are both mammals, whereas in terms of functional entailment it is said that "dogs chase rabbits". Taxonomic classification is logically more powerful and necessary for making conceptual distinctions, but the answer that dogs chase rabbits is not stupid or pre-logical, and perfectly sensible in the context of ordinary life.

So when intuitive thinkers are asked to classify a variety of things, they put them in clusters of things that "go" or "belong" together, so that knives, forks, and spoons will be included with tables and chairs, and with food and drink, because they all go naturally together for a meal in what we can call a "complex". In the same way, models of cow, pig, house, and man, "go" together because he is a farmer. A good example is from Dahomey, where the goddess Mawu represents the female principle, and therefore fertility, motherhood, gentleness, and forgiveness; while the god Lisa represents power (warlike or otherwise), strength and toughness. They are also associated with day and night: Mawu is the night, the moon, freshness, rest, and joy; while Lisa is the day, the sun, heat, labour, and all hard things (Forde 1954:219).

These are extremely practical ways of ordering the world, based on the associations between features of daily life, but this sort of classification can't form the basis of taxonomic classes. Examples of what we call taxonomic classes are "utensil", "vehicle", and "furniture", because they are based on some common characteristic, regardless of their associations in ordinary life, and are characteristic of formal operational thought. Someone might ask, however, why we should care about taxonomic classes in the first place. While they are unnecessary in primitive society, they are a very powerful way of ordering experience, and advanced legal and administrative systems, logic, and all scientific thought, would be impossible without them.

They are formed by abstracting certain criteria from all their associations in real life and making them the defining criteria of a particular class. Take, for example, our taxonomic concept of "vehicle"; we are not concerned with how expensive it is, or if it is kept in a garage, or who drives it, or what makes it go, but only with the minimal defining features: "A means of conveyance provided with wheels or runners and used for the carriage of persons or goods". So one of the defining criteria of a vehicle is that it runs along the ground (whether on wheels, runners, or tracks), and as such it is in a different class from boats or aeroplanes. We can further distinguish between different sub-classes of vehicles as "cars" or "trucks", and sub-classes of, say, cars by their makes. These are all "taxonomic" or logical classes and they are not only defined by clear criteria but also form a hierarchy from the general to the increasingly particular:

They are fundamental for the development of formal-operational thought: for administration, logic, philosophy and, ultimately, for science. For example, in this hierarchy the class A is divided into sub-classes B, C, and D, and D in turn is divided into sub-sub-classes E and F, and so on. In other words, we can understand a hierarchy of logical classes as a system of class inclusions, so that class A>D>F>H, and therefore that A>H. We express these inclusions by use of the logical concepts of "all", "some", and "none" (e.g. *all* members of F are only *some* of D, *no* E is F, *some* F is *all* H and so on).

But someone who does not understand the logic of class inclusion and logical "all", "some", and "none" will not be able to understand certain forms of reasoning involving logical proof. For example, if someone tells us that *all* animals in Australia are marsupials, and that the koala bear is an Australian animal, we accept as a matter of *logic* that therefore the koala must also be a marsupial, even if we have never been to Australia and know nothing about the animals that live there. We can understand the idea of logical proof as distinct from factual truth, but this is a sophisticated, formal-operational distinction that would be quite unfamiliar to anyone in a pre-literate society. They would reject the suggestion that the koala must be a marsupial precisely because they had not been to Australia, and therefore could not be expected to know anything about the animals there (Luria 1976:117–121). The whole idea that statements are not just about facts, or expressions of feelings, but can also be taken as having a logical form and so can be proved, regardless of whether they are actually true in the real world, originally occurred to people in Greece, India, and China less than 2500 years ago. These were groups of specialist thinkers who spent a great deal of time arguing about philosophy and religion, and how society should be organised, and they all discovered the need to be able to analyse the force of each other's arguments simply as arguments, and to find some objective way of disproving them. But for most of history, and for most cultures, logic in this sense has certainly not been available as a mode of thought.

4. The mind and the world

Initially, at the intuitive stage of thought, children have no understanding of the mind, or of how it relates to the body, and a good example is how they come to understand the significance of speech and words. At the first stage, when the child can even understand the meaning of the question (at about 6), he supposes that we think with the mouth when we speak, and also identifies thoughts with breath, air, and smoke, or else equates thinking with hearing and so regards this as something we do with our ears. Words, and especially names, are regarded as a part of the things they refer to, and the function of the ears and mouth is therefore limited to collaborating with things—receiving words and sending them out. Words themselves therefore have strength, or weight, or speed, or any other property of the thing referred to. At the first stage, therefore, there are two related confusions—between thinking and the body, and between the sign or the word and what it signifies.

The development of the understanding of names is particularly revealing, for "name" is a much clearer concept for the child than "word" (and was certainly true for the Konso and the Tauade). At the first stage, when the child learns the name of something, he supposes that he is thereby reaching to the essence of that thing and discovering some real kind of explanation of what it is like. Things did not exist before they had names or, if a name exists there must be something in the real world to which it corresponds. Because names are properties of things, they are discoverable and we can come to know the names of things just by looking at them.

At the stage of concrete operations, names are supposed to have been given to things by God, or by the first men, but may still be thought in a sense to be "in the things" or else as being "everywhere and nowhere". Even if we can't recognise a thing's name when we see it, the child still supposes that there is an inherent "rightness" about names—the word "sun" involves "shining, round, etc". The child can now understand that there is a problem about the relation between words and things, but still fails to solve it. Only at the third, formal, stage does he come to realise that names are just conventional labels, handed down by tradition. They are progressively understood to be located in the voice, in the head, and then in thought itself, which has now come to be located in the head as an unobservable and immaterial process. (Plato, in the *Cratylus*, has a long discussion about whether names are natural or conventional, and would not have done so unless at least some of his contemporaries had been puzzled by the question.)

It is also at the stage of formal operations that the child finally begins to understand the adult concept of the mind in general, and that thought is a set of representations conveyed in language. Our notion of the mind is therefore not obvious to all normal human beings: it has been constructed very laboriously by thinkers and scientists only in the last few thousand or even hundreds of years of literate civilisation, and we can only grasp it because we live in a complex society with an advanced technology, and have had many years of schooling and literacy. Schooling in our society requires children to explain their reasons for making particular choices in test situations, demands that they give reasons and justifications for beliefs, and challenges to the individual's own point of view in debate and argument ("That's just your opinion—how do you know?"), so that schooling in particular develops the awareness of one's own mental processes and the ability to talk about them.

But in primitive society children do not have the opportunity to be challenged about the nature of names and language in these ways because there is no formal schooling. Whereas children in our society learn in the artificial environment of the school where they have to solve problems that are outside their ordinary experience, and engage in debate, in primitive society the child is gradually introduced into the full life of an adult, "and is almost never told what to do in an explicit, verbal, or abstract manner. He is expected to watch, learning by imitation and repetition [in the context of ordinary life so that] education is concrete and nonverbal, concerned with practical activity, not abstract generalisation. There are never lectures on farming, house-building, or weaving. the child spends all his days watching until at some point he is told to join in the activity" (Gay & Cole 1967:16). The object of education is not cleverness, or to question or experiment or to think for oneself, but good sense, wisdom, and the ability to perform as a good neighbour and kinsman in work and social relations. The child is highly motivated to conform, and his basic learning commitment is not to things or ideas, but to people, especially those closest to him socially.

As a result, our notion of the mind does not develop in primitive society. For example:

The Dinka [of the Sudan] have no conception which at all closely corresponds to our popular modern conception of the "mind", as mediating and, as it were, storing up the experiences of the self. There is for them no such interior entity to appear, on reflection, to stand between the experiencing self at any given moment and what is or has been an exterior influence upon the self. So it seems that what we should call in some cases "the memories" of experiences, and regard therefore as in some way intrinsic and interior to the remembering person and modified in their effect upon him by that interiority, appear to the

Dinka as exteriorly acting upon him, as were the sources from which they derived. Hence it would be impossible to suggest to Dinka that a powerful dream was "only" a dream, and might for that reason be dismissed as relatively unimportant in the light of day, or that a state of possession was grounded "merely" in the psychology of the person possessed. They do not make the kind of distinction between the psyche and the world which would make such interpretations significant for them (Lienhardt 1961:149).

The early Greeks identified thought with breath, and speech and thinking with the lungs (Onians 1954:13, 67–68), and for the Trobriand Islanders:

The mind, nanola, by which term intelligence, power of discrimination, capacity for learning magical formulae and all forms of non-manual skill are described, as well as moral qualities resides somewhere in the larynx. The natives will always point to the organs of speech, where the nanola resides. The man who cannot speak through any defect of his organs, is identified in name and treatment with all those mentally deficient (Malinowski 1922:408–9).

And among the Gahuku-Gama, "cognitive processes are associated with the organs of hearing. To 'know' or to 'think' is to 'hear'; 'I don't know' or 'I don't understand' is 'I do not hear' or 'I have not heard'" (Read 1955:265), just as with the Tauade. The lack of a distinct notion of the mind is also related to a lack of a distinct notion of the body, and leads to a combination of the mental and the physical in what Read calls a physiological psychology:

The biological, physiological and psychic aspect of man's nature cannot be clearly separated. They exist in the closest inter-dependence, being, as it were, fused together to form the human personality. To an extent to which it is perhaps difficult for us to appreciate or understand, the various parts of the body, limbs, eyes, nose, hair, the internal organs and bodily excretions are essential constituents of the human personality, incorporating and expressing the whole in each of their several functions. It follows that an injury to any part of the body is also comparable to damage to the personality of the individual sustaining the injury. Similarly, the loss of any of the bodily substances through excretion is, in a rather obscure sense, the loss of something that is an essential part or element of the whole, a loss to the personality itself (Read 1955:265).

They will still be "connected" to their owner, which is why burning a man's hair clippings, for example, will seem a reasonable method of inflicting real physical harm on him.

Once we realise that primitive peoples do not have our idea of the mind we can also understand why they will inevitably think of all the symbols used in their rituals, the water, the garlands, the sacred gates, and so on as having real supernatural power. When we talk of "symbolic meaning" we can use our notion of "mind" to make a clear distinction between the symbol and what it stands for. So when we see an object that has symbolic power, such as our national flag, we regard our feelings about it as existing in our minds and not in the flag itself. But our notion of the mind is not available to primitive man, so for him the power of the symbol can only be located in the object itself.

Again, when we see a picture of someone we know, we think of the associations conjured up by seeing the familiar face as located in our mind. But suppose we had no idea of the mind, of the processing centre that brings together visual impressions and the memories of this person? Then what else could we do but locate those feelings in the picture itself, and think of them as existing outside us, and of the picture as having a mysterious life of its own? The same is true of symbols used in rituals, and also of speech, when, for example, spells are uttered, and the words associated with the things named in the spell are thought to be under the control of the words that are spoken.

So ritual, and the words used in magical spells, curses, and blessings are not just *expressing* peoples' hopes and fears: they are actually creating a new reality, as when a Tauade believes that saying the name of a strong local wind will make him as swift as that wind in battle, or that another spell will make his journey shorter. Against this background, therefore, magic and witchcraft will have far more credibility than they can possess in our kind of society.

Intuitive thought also makes no clear distinction between natural and social laws:

…until the age of 7–8 there does not exist for the child a single purely mechanical law of nature. If clouds move swiftly when the wind is blowing, this is not only because of a necessary connection between the movement of the wind and that of the clouds; it is also and primarily because the clouds "must" hurry along to bring us rain, or night, and so on…. If boats remain afloat on the water while stones sink to the bottom, this does not happen merely for reasons relating to their weight; it is because things have to be so in virtue of the World-Order. In short, the universe is permeated with moral rules; physical regularity is not dissociated from moral obligation and social rule…. What, then, do intentions matter? The problem of responsibility is simply to know whether a law has been respected or violated. Just as if we trip, independently of any carelessness, we fall to the ground by virtue of the law of gravity, so tampering with the truth, even unwittingly, will be called a lie and incur punishment. If the fault remains unnoticed, things themselves will take charge of punishing us (Piaget 1952:429–430).

A boy, for example, has been stealing apples and on the way home falls into a stream because the bridge breaks; he will believe that the bridge broke *because* he had been stealing apples (Piaget 1970:250).

Since the social and natural worlds are not clearly distinguished, the most elementary way to explain physical phenomena is based, naturally enough, on how people behave. People act for a purpose, and because of their inner, essential nature, and so intuitive thinkers suppose that the movement of an object expresses the force or vitality inside it, and also that this vitality is purposeful and goal directed. "Every substance is endowed with a *sui generis* force, unacquired and untransmissible, constituting the very essence of its activity…. If we try to find out exactly what a child means when he says that a force sets an object in motion, we always discover the idea of mutual excitation." That is, the movement of a body is regarded as due both to an external will and to an internal will, to command and to obedience. There is no *transmission* of force: "the external force simply calls forth the internal force which belongs to the moving object", as when a child says, "The road makes the bicycles go" (Piaget 1930:118–19). The movement of things such as clouds and streams, for example, is seen as inherent in them, and called forth by what they have to do in the scheme of things. The child does not think, then, as we do, of force being transmitted from body to body but as belonging to all bodies, not transmitted but awakened—the weight of a stone, for example, is regarded as a force that actively opposes the efforts of a person to lift it. (Thomas Kuhn, for example (1957:96–7) points out some resemblances between Aristotle's ideas of motion and those of primitives and children.)

Intuitive thought therefore thinks of cause and effect much more easily in terms of essences than as the result of relations between objects. The shadow, for example, is not understood as the result of a beam of light from a light-source that is obstructed by an object, and casts a projection of this on to the ground, but as something that emerges from inside the person or object that casts it, a thing that has its own special properties. The fact that a shadow can't be seen in cloudy conditions or at night does not conflict with this belief, because it is supposed that the shadow is still there but is just temporarily invisible. Since a shadow is therefore a special kind of thing, the shadows of people, in particular, are often supposed to be related to the soul, or at least vulnerable to magic or witchcraft. For the same reason, in primitive thought darkness itself is not regarded simply as the absence of light, but as something existing as a separate kind of thing in its own right.

The properties of objects, including people, may also be seen as something that can be transmitted directly between people and objects, and such beliefs are universal in primitive society. So if travellers are very tired on a long journey and fanning themselves with leaves, they may throw the leaves away in the belief that that their tiredness will leave them and pass into the leaves. A mother may not let her children eat the flesh of a species of white-bearded monkey because she thinks that they will catch old age from it. When a tree does not bear fruit, a gardener may ask a pregnant woman to fasten a stone to one of its branches, so that her fertility will pass into the tree, and so on.

The intuitive idea of causes, therefore, is a universe of independent and spontaneous substances that behave as they do because of their essential natures, but it is also a universe in which these substances are linked by their concrete associations in the experiences of everyday life. These "realms of experience", such as the bush, the forest, the village, the lowlands, and so on are complexes that may come to be regarded as having some kind of inner vitality of their own. Among the Dinka of the Sudan, for example, there are three divinities who are thought of as a family: Garang the father, Abuk the wife, and Deng as son or husband of Abuk. Deng represents the phenomena of the sky associated with rain, and hence also rain-clouds, thunder, lighting, and sudden death and also, by association, coolness, pastures, cattle, milk, procreation, abundance, light, and life. Abuk is a female divinity who presides over women's affairs: gardens, crops and food, and the earth generally, while Garang represents the heat of the sun and certain heated conditions of the human body.

Since the primitive world is filled with purpose and meaning, there is no room for our notions of probability and accident in explaining why things happen For example, if a tree falls on a man and kills him, people will obviously understand, physically speaking, what caused his death but they will also want to know why the tree fell on him, in particular, and not on someone else, or why it killed anyone at all. Because the world has meaning, any event with human significance must have an explanation, and it is only in the case of an insignificant event, such as a tree simply falling down without doing any damage, that they will say, "It just happened". Such beliefs are the easier to hold because people also have no ability to think statistically, that is, to think about events in numerical terms and understand that the larger the number of cases, the more likely it is that accidents or deaths will occur.

For example, I used to treat the members of the Konso towns where I lived for a variety of complaints such as conjunctivitis, dysentery, cuts and burns, in which I was very successful. This was because the complaints were not serious and the people reacted well to modern antibiotics, but a number of people would never go to the Mission clinic and insisted on coming to me, because they said the clinic was a bad place where people died, whereas they had never known me to fail. They simply compared the *absolute* success rates of myself and the clinic instead of our *relative* success rates, relative, that is, to the far greater number of patients treated by the clinic, some of whom were also much more seriously ill than any I saw, and more likely to die in any case. The assumption that significant events must have a meaning in the larger scheme of things, and the inability to think statistically, form, of course, the basis of the universal belief in omens and divination. (Piaget found that, in the same way, children find it natural to think of events as inherently linked together in patterns and only develop an understanding of probability with great difficulty at the stage of formal operations.)

From what we have now seen of the basic features of intuitive or pre-operational thought, it is obvious that it provides major support for all those beliefs in ritual, magic, witchcraft, divination, spirits and nature-gods and goddesses for which anthropologists and biologists have tried to find adaptive explanations.

5. Social and moral ideas

Primitive peoples find it just as difficult to think analytically about their own societies as they do about the physical world or about themselves. Of course they know the practical details of how their own society works, but this knowledge can't be expressed in an articulate and coherent way. In small groups, which continue for generation after generation in the same place, with a simple technology, it is very easy to develop rules (such as those for kinship and marriage) based on principles that do not necessarily have to be made explicit. Small changes can be made in each generation which will fit in with the general pattern of life, but this "fitting in" need not require a conscious awareness of the whole pattern. The symbolic links between the natural world and the clans and lineages, age groups, men's societies, and the rituals associated with these in tribal society also make conscious analysis of one's own social order very difficult.

The organisation of Tauade society, for example, can be summarised in a page, but none of my informants could provide me with any description of their society at all which summed up its main institutions. In one sense the Tauade knew perfectly well how their society was organised, but this knowledge was based on a great mass of concrete personal information about individuals whom they knew and their relationships with them. It would therefore have been impossible for a Tauade to have put this type of knowledge into a connected set of general statements about their social organisation and the relations between tribes, clans, lineages, hamlets, Big Men, and so on. In the same way, moral ideas are thoroughly embedded in social life and not discussed in any general way, so that we don't find words for "justice", "duty", "virtue", "rights", or "moral" in the languages of primitive societies.

Many anthropological studies such as Hobhouse 1929, Ginsberg 1944, Read 1955, Kluckhohn 1960, von Fürer-Haimendorf 1967, and Hallpike 2016, have made it clear from their studies of primitive society that there has been an evolutionary development in the way that people have thought about moral issues. Some of their more notable conclusions about the slow emergence of formal operational or Principled moral thinking in literate civilisation are as follows:

1. The range of moral concern has steadily extended from one's immediate kin and neighbours to include human beings in general. "The best established trend is the extension of the range of persons to whom moral judgements apply; it is not so much the sense of duty to a neighbour that had varied as the answer to the question who is my neighbour" (Ginsberg 1944:19).

2. The concept of duty is initially bound up with group membership and the performance of specific social roles. "In the early stages of ethics rights and duties do not attach to a human being as such. They attach to him as a member of a group" (Hobhouse 1929:233). Only much later does it become the general principle of moral obligation, in which it becomes possible to think of other people as individual moral beings regardless of their social status.

3. The most elementary concept of justice is that of equal exchange, of reciprocity, of good for good and bad for bad. Only in more complex societies does it develop more fully into concepts of social fairness, and an explicit notion of the Golden Rule and mentally taking the place of others.

4. There is therefore a general development from conventional to principled morality. One aspect of this is a growing distinction between the duties of custom and law, on one hand, and those of a purely moral nature on the other, between social conventions and basic ethical principles. This is related to the ability to think about society as a whole and to criticise it on general moral grounds such as justice. Another aspect of the development of

principled morality is the kind of justification for doing what is right. "There gradually emerges the notion that goodness is something which the mind can apprehend as self-sustained and independent of external sanctions. Among simpler peoples, as described by anthropologists, the sanctions behind customary rules are relatively external and prudential" (Ginsberg 1944:23).

5. This process is related to another major dimension of moral development that has been observed by anthropologists and historians, which is the growing awareness of the inner life of the individual, and of the mind in its cognitive aspects, as necessary to understand why other people behave as they do, and how it would feel to be in their place. So we find a development from objective to subjective responsibility, from a predominant concern with the act and its consequences towards the recognition of subjective factors of motive and intention on the part of the agent. This development is closely related to a further aspect of moral development, from a morality of *shame*, the consciousness that one has offended against an external, social rule, to that of *guilt*, an inner conviction of wrong-doing with its essential element of self-condemnation by one's conscience.

6. Another aspect of this growing awareness of the inner life of the mind is a clearer articulation of the idea of virtue in relation to the self. Members of primitive societies can easily give lists of what are regarded as desirable qualities—generosity, bravery, good temper, and so on—and these are remarkably similar cross-culturally. But there is no analysis of the essential elements of character that allow people to perform well as moral agents, such as the cardinal virtues of Plato and Aristotle; the virtues in primitive societies are simply lists of personal qualities that remain unsynthesised, a "bag of virtues", as Kohlberg has described them.

Many developmental psychologists, notably Piaget's *The Moral Judgment of the Child* (1970), Kohlberg's *The Psychology of Moral Development* (1984), and many other studies (see Snarey 1985), have traced how social and moral understanding develops in the individual from childhood onwards. In assessing the development of moral understanding it has become clear that this cannot be understood in isolation from the way in which social understanding as a whole develops, because obviously moral action takes place in a social context.

Initially, children conceive social relations as between concrete individuals, rather than as a structure of roles, and indeed there is great difficulty in constructing representations of stable roles. Conventions are rigid but uncoordinated, and are to be obeyed without consideration of why they exist. Interpersonal behaviour is strongly dependent on the fear of consequences, and the predominant notion of what is right is that of reciprocity or fair exchange. In assessing responsibility attention focuses on acts rather than on motives or intentions, moral judgments are relative to which particular people are involved, while the idea of the self is based on one's own actions and physical categories of identity, such as gender and age.

Following this, social relations come to be represented not just as relations between concrete individuals, but also in terms of group membership. Loyalty to groups such as family, friends, and neighbours, and the opinions of these groups are the basis of conventions of right and wrong, so that people are anxious to have good reputations for living up to what is expected of them. Political authority is seen as belonging to certain archetypal figures of importance and power, like fathers or elders; social convention and moral rules are not clearly distinguished so that what is customary is what is good. Then gradually society comes to be understood in a more concrete-operational and systematic manner, and hierarchical structures and role differences are understood more clearly. An example of this would be an understanding of the structure and working of a political system or an administrative organisation. What is right consists in maintaining the society as a whole, and more distinction is made between intentions and actions when awarding punishment. This develops into a more systemically coordinated representation of society as an ordered system, with authority as a hierarchy of roles that are also differentiated in function. People have the duty of maintaining the system as a whole and contributing to the common good. Law is necessary for this common good, as is political authority, and law and justice are the basis of morality.

Finally, especially in literate civilisations such as our own, at a stage corresponding to formal operations, some adolescents are able to transcend the limitations of their particular society and think of it as only one among a number of possible types. One's own society can become the subject of criticism, and hypothetical social orders discussed. Moral principles become distinguished from the customary and the legal and are recognised as valid in their own right. The individual can be thought of as such, distinct from his or her actual social position. The individual is therefore distinguished from society, and it becomes possible to think of moral obligations to all human beings, regardless of the society to which they belong. Customs are now seen as conventions that are justified by their contribution to the smooth working of society, rather than as simply good or mandatory in themselves, and law and morality are distinguished. The self is primarily defined in psychological and spiritual terms, and is much more differentiated and integrated, with physical attributes of relatively less importance. There is also a clear awareness of the mind as mediating between one's experiences of the world and one's inner representations of it. The cognitive functions of the mind are therefore realised, and the self can be the judge of the self, so that the idea of conscience is fully developed. Correspondingly, in assessing the moral and legal responsibility of others, their motives and intentions, as well as their actions, are taken into account. The idea of justice has advanced to the principle of the Golden Rule: doing to others as one would like them to do to us.

We can sum up this general development of moral ideas, very briefly, as involving the ability to form an increasingly coherent grasp of social systems; to reflect on one's own inner states and those of others; to think of others independently of their specific social status as moral beings in their own right, and therefore an increasingly equilibrated grasp of the relations between society and the individual, in all of which the opportunities for mutual perspective-taking and discussion are of great importance. In this process, ideas about sanctions and responsibility, obligation, moral principles, the self, and the virtues form parts of a mutually reinforcing system of ideas. While this type of Principled thinking is standard for educated people in literate civilisations, many people even in our own industrialised societies do not attain this level of thought, and it certainly does not occur at all in tribal society. All of this, of course, is impossible to square with the belief of sociobiologists like Hauser that we have an ethical module that was selected for when our remote ancestors were Pleistocene hunter-gatherers in East Africa.

6. Social experience and cognitive development

In the Darwinian scheme of things the organism by itself is only capable of random variation, and so is basically passive in relation to the environment, which imposes itself on the organism through selection. As Skinner put it, "A person does not act on the world, the world acts upon him". But I have constantly stressed the importance of human *activity* in exploring the possibilities of the natural and the cultural worlds, and this has also been a basic theme of developmental psychology. So the cultural world both moulds human consciousness, and is moulded by it, and this is not only true of collective representations, but of the cognitive growth of individuals. The cognitive development of concrete and formal operations in the understanding of the physical world is closely related to the cultural opportunities that have been available in the course of human history, and is still continuing.

It is very well established, for example, that since 1900 at least, scores in IQ tests have steadily risen in all the developed nations of the western world—the "Flynn effect"—and these tests include success at Piagetian tasks. Many studies find that children who do not attend school score drastically lower on the tests than those who attend school regularly. "Formal schooling is highly correlated with Piagetian progress. Today's 14-year-olds live at a time in which they have had nine years of formal schooling with more to come. In the America of 1900, adults had an average of about seven years of schooling ... and 25 percent had completed four years or less.... And it was schooling of much inferior quality" (Flynn 2007:32). There has not only been a great extension of secondary education, but of university education as well, so that whereas in 1960 when I was an undergraduate around 5% of the British population went to university, now it is closer to 50%. The general environment during that period has also become much more complex and stimulating, in particular the need and opportunity to master an ever more demanding technology in every sphere of life. Again, one of the most striking 20th-century changes of the human intellectual environment has come from the increase of exposure to many types of visual media. From pictures on the wall to movies to television to video games to computers, each successive generation has been exposed to richer optical displays than the one before and may have become more adept at visual analysis. Environmental changes resulting from modernisation—such as more intellectually demanding work, greater use of technology and smaller families—have meant that a much larger proportion of people are more accustomed to manipulating abstract concepts such as hypotheses and categories than a century ago. Substantial portions of IQ tests deal with these abilities.

The same interactive relationship between the individual and the cultural environment is also true of cognitive growth in social and moral understanding. We have already seen that development of the concepts of space, time, physical causality, and classification is hindered by the very simple forms of life and technology in primitive society, and the same is true of the development of social and moral ideas. These conclusions of developmental psychologists and anthropologists show that the development of moral ideas is a highly complex process and closely related to social experience. Cross-cultural studies confirm that there are certain features of social experience which retard cognitive development in moral thinking and others that stimulate it. Life in small, isolated, homogeneous rural communities, with lack of formal education and literacy, lack of participation in a monetary economy, lack of participation in leadership roles and in state-level institutions, and lack of experience of cultural diversity, are all retarding influences, in particular because of their limited opportunities for *encountering different social perspectives.*

On the other hand, it has been found that interaction with non-kin in an urban environment, engagement in commercial relations, the experience of cultural diversity, acting as community leaders, or participating in state level institutions, all generate higher levels of cognitive functioning. These higher levels of moral thinking involve in particular *an enhanced degree of mutual perspective-taking.* "A variety of evidence across the data bases is consistent with the cognitive developmental expectation that moral judgment stage development is facilitated by social perspective-taking opportunities" (Gibbs 2007:489–90). They also found that "diverse social experiences foster the development of more adequate psychological understandings or 'theories' of mind (one's own and others'), and that it is the person's theory of mind that then undergirds the moral judgment gain" (ibid., 490). It will also be obvious that all the stimulating factors associated with mutual perspective-taking are inherently associated with those features of societal complexity which have evolved in the course of history and are not found at the simpler levels of social organisation.

Other cognitively stimulating activities such as planning, co-ordination, differences of opinion and debate, and settlement of legal disputes become specially important with emergence of the state. This greatly intensifies the degree of conscious, rational thought for organising tax collection and public works, planning conquest warfare, legal and theological debate, commercial calculations, and, with the advent of literacy, schooling. Literacy combined with mere rote learning, as in the scribal schools of ancient Egypt and Mesopotamia, has no significant cognitive consequences, but schooling and formal education that involve taking the pupils out of the context of their normal daily lives and their active participation and discussion with their teachers is of particular importance. It is closely involved with the ability to explain verbally one's reasons for making particular choices in test situations, and it also seems to develop the search for rules for the solution of problems, and the awareness of one's own mental operations. It is not surprising that social facilities for public debate which developed in the ancient civilisations were essential to the emergence of philosophy.

While there is therefore a general correlation between the historical and the psychological development of moral thinking, this cannot be explained as a process by which growing social complexity is simply reflected in growing psychological complexity imprinted on the minds of individuals. On the contrary, there has to be a dialectical relationship between the social environment and the *psychological* factors of individuals.

7. Conclusions

These revolutionary developments in the power of human thought were not, then, the result of any changes in our genes and our basic intelligence, but of the co-evolution of culture and the cognitive abilities of the individuals who transmitted it. Developmental psychology *alone* can't, of course, explain the process by which human understanding has evolved in the course of human history. For example, a shift to agriculture is not the result of any new cognitive process, but by producing much larger social groups and new forms of property relations it also leads to a new range of problems and dilemmas which do involve cognitive change. In the same way the emergence of the state, or money and the predominance of commercial transactions, or law courts, or industrialisation do not require, as such, some new cognitive ability, but they are likely to bring about new social conditions which provide a more cognitively demanding social environment. The use of developmental psychology therefore allows us to go beyond the static Durkheimian correlations between social organisation and collective representations because it focuses on the dynamic problems that real individuals have to deal with in grasping their world and which change their modes of thought.

Notes

1. E. O. Wilson unfortunately thought that "genetic epistemology" must be all about genes: "Piaget, who was originally trained as a biologist, views intellectual development as an interaction of an inherited genetic programme with the environment. It is no coincidence that he calls this conception 'genetic epistemology', in effect the study of the hereditary unfolding of understanding." (2004:66–7). This displays a total misunderstanding of Piaget, who thought nothing of the kind, and for whom "genetic epistemology" meant "the genesis or origin of knowledge".

2. Gregory Forth, on the other hand, in his study of time concepts of the Rindi in eastern Sumba, provides a good example of what does seem a genuine example of a concrete-operational grasp of time in a primitive society. The Rindi have institutional horse-racing on a circular track, and this involves a system of handicaps for horses of different sizes—and therefore speeds. In this system, the larger horses have to run farther than smaller horses, and therefore start at different points around the track, the largest ones in fact going almost twice as far as the smallest. While the race does not end at the same instant, because all the horses start simultaneously this handicapping arrangement, as he says, "evidently entails the realisation that larger horses will be able to run faster, and, more

importantly in the present context, that within the same period of time, faster (i.e. larger) horses will be able to cover a greater distance", so that "in the eastern Sumbanese horse race 'distance covered' or 'work done' appears indeed to be dissociated from 'time elapsed'" (Forth 1982:245). He does not claim that this is the dominant mode of time-reckoning in their society, but it is a good illustration of how familiarity with particular activities may involve the development of concrete-operational thinking. In other respects, however, he records that Rindi collective representations of time generally conform to the spatialized time typical of primitive society.

Chapter V
The new biology

It will have become obvious that the constructivist account I have given of cultural evolution inhabits an entirely different thought-world from that of Natural Selection, and this should hardly be surprising since cultural processes are very different from those of biology. But since I have maintained that neo-Darwinian theory cannot apply to cultural evolution it would be all the same to me if it had been shown to be correct down to the smallest detail in explaining biological evolution. In fact, however, neo-Darwinism has actually been increasingly challenged by major developments in evolutionary biology since *The Selfish Gene* was published in 1976. "A major paradigm shift is currently underway in evolutionary theory. Neo-Darwinism—the reductionist, mechanistic, gene-centred approach to evolution epitomised by the selfish gene metaphor of Richard Dawkins—has come under assault from various quarters" (Corning 2005:1). The revolution includes the acceptance of multi-level selection theory and the renewed emphasis on the importance of the organism and of group selection, the rise of epigenetics, evolutionary-developmental biology ("evo-devo") with its emphasis on self-organisation in particular, lateral gene transfer, symbiosis, neutralism, and major developments in mathematical biology especially with the use of computers.

The sequencing of the human genome completed in 2003 has also produced many surprises. When Dawkins wrote *The Selfish Gene* he was well aware that "a large fraction of the DNA is never translated into protein", so-called "junk" DNA, and that "Biologists are racking their brains trying to think what useful task this apparently surplus DNA is doing…. The simplest way to explain the surplus DNA is to suppose that it is a parasite, or at best a harmless but useless passenger…" (ibid., 47). But the sequencing of the human genome made it clear that around 98% of human DNA does not actually code for proteins, rather a lot of junk, to put it mildly. It might have seemed rather implausible that natural selection would have preserved so much useless material at the heart of inheritance, and in fact the rise of epigenetics has shown that much of this "junk" DNA is not junk at all but contains elaborate instructions for the construction of the organism and so is essential for reproduction:

> *Some of it forms specific structures in the chromosomes, the enormous molecules into which our DNA is packaged. This junk prevents our DNA from unravelling and becoming damaged…. Yet others act as insulating regions, restricting gene expression to specific regions of chromosomes…. But a great deal of our junk DNA is not simply structural. It doesn't code for proteins, but it does code for a different type of molecule, called RNA. A large class of this junk DNA forms factories in the cell, helping to produce proteins. Other types of RNA molecules transport the raw material for protein production to the factory sites. [But] A major role of junk DNA, only recognised in the main in the last few years, is to regulate gene expression. Sometimes this can have a huge and noticeable effect in an individual…. Thousands and thousands of regions of junk DNA are suspected to regulate networks of gene expression (Carey 2015:4–5).*

The other shock from the sequencing of the human genome was the realisation that the extraordinary complexities of human anatomy, physiology, intelligence and behaviour cannot be explained by referring to the classical model of genes. In terms of numbers of genes that code for proteins, humans contain pretty much the same quantity (around 20,000) as simple microscopic worms. Even more remarkably, most of the genes in the worms have directly equivalent genes in humans.

As researchers deepened their analyses of what differentiates humans from other organisms at the DNA level, it became apparent that genes could not provide the explanation. In fact, only one genetic factor generally scaled with complexity. The only genomic features that increased in number as animals became more complex were the regions of junk DNA. The more sophisticated an organism, the higher percentage of junk DNA it contains (ibid., 4).

Stated simply, then, the body is not a mere vehicle for the genes, as Dawkins claims, and his notion of genes as independent replicators that determine more less everything about us was exaggerated at the time and is now even more obsolete, since we know that DNA in general, not just genes, cannot replicate independently of the cell:

> *It replicates accurately only in a complete cell containing all the objective functionality that enable cells to be alive. Cells achieve this outcome through a very complicated three-stage process in which the millions of errors are detected and corrected.... Those processes rely on an army of specialised proteins and on the lipid membranous structures for which there are no DNA sequences. Outside a living cell, DNA is inert, dead. The living functionality is crucial (Noble 2018:248).*

And,

> *Process structuralists view genes not as controllers or regulators of ontogeny and morphology but as important players in complex developmental processes. In these processes genes interact with RNA, proteins, and other organic macromolecules in such a way that different molecules in this complex developmental system can regulate each other. For instance, genes can code for proteins, but proteins, genes, and other macromolecules can regulate gene expression. Thus, ontogeny is not simply the unfolding of some genetic program; it is*

> *a complex process that has its own patterns and its own momen-*
> *tum. The genome constitutes a part of a parallel processing network*
> *composed of many different molecules (Kauffman, 1995) (Resnik*
> *1994:8).*

If genes were never the independent "replicators" depicted by Dawkins the memes never had a plausible biological model to give them even minimal credibility in the first place. So it is remarkable, after the revolutionary developments which have taken place in biology since *The Selfish Gene* was first published, that Dawkins makes scarcely any mention of these advances in *The Extended Selfish Gene*, published in 2016, and even his highly criticised notion of the meme is reproduced entirely unchanged forty years later. The notion of the meme has been the subject of intense, critical discussion such as in Orr 1996, Pinker 1997, Aunger 2000, Sperber 2000, Laland and Brown 2002, Richerson and Boyd 2006, and Hallpike 1986, 2011, and Pinker in particular might seem to demand a response since he is a sociobiologist who does not accept the idea of the meme. Dawkins's 2016 notes updating his thinking on the meme refer instead to errors in versions of Auld Lang Syne, memes as neuronal patterns in the brain, the growing popularity of Hamilton's notion of kin selection, computer viruses, an attack on religious faith, and a denial that he is a genetic determinist. None of these topics suggests that he is willing to respond to the serious objections to the theory of the meme that have been advanced over the last forty years.

The claim of Universal Darwinism that mutation and selection is the *only* mechanism of evolution has also been disproved because the importance of a fundamentally different mode of evolution involving what is known as lateral gene transfer has also been established, particularly by the work of Lynn Margulis and her predecessors on symbiosis who had been ignored for many years. We now know that for around 2 billion years the only life-form consisted of bacteria (prokaryotes), which were able (and of course still are capable) of exchanging their genes directly, in a combinatorial process in addition to mutational changes:

> *[Prokaryotes]…engage in what is called horizontal (or lateral) gene transfer. We've known that prokaryotic cells can exchange DNA with one another since the early 1950s … but no one could have predicted the extent of their promiscuity. Analysis of prokaryotic genomes show them to be complex mosaics of genes taken from here, there, and everywhere, often with blatant disregard for species boundaries. All this mixing and matching has led researchers to vigorously debate the relative importance of vertical and horizontal gene flow in prokaryotic evolution, and to question whether prokaryotic species even exist (Archibald 2016:29–30).*

Furthermore, every cell of plants and animals ("eukaryotic" cells) has within it many small bodies known as "organelles". Some of these are *mitochondria*, which are responsible for producing the energy the cell needs for its various functions, and others are *chloroplasts*, in which plants use photosynthesis for food and energy. It has been definitively established that:

> *These organelles once used to be free-living bacteria that, around 2 billion years ago, entered some of the first eukaryotic life forms through phagocytosis (eating or engulfment). The organisms engaged in symbiosis, this became permanent and hereditary, and the once free-living organisms evolved into the organelles.… The bacterial lineages wherefrom mitochondria and chloroplasts evolved still exist as free-living bacteria today… (Gontier 2016:261).*

This theory of symbiogenesis was vigorously opposed by orthodox neo-Darwinians, but was conclusively proved to be correct when it was established that mitochondrial DNA was different from the DNA of the host cell.

It is also maintained that symbiogenesis was responsible for the development of the eukaryotic cell itself, which has a distinct nucleus containing the DNA. "According to Margulis, the nucleated cell also evolved by means of symbiogenesis. As such, it was symbiogenesis that enabled both the evolutionary transition from prokaryotes to eukaryotes, and the subsequent evolution of the four eukaryotic kingdoms" [plants, animals, fungi, and single celled organisms like algae] (Gontier 2016:261). The eukaryotic cell, therefore, was absolutely fundamental in evolution because it was essential to the emergence of all the plants, animals and other complex multi-cellular life-forms with which we are familiar, but mutation and selection by themselves are quite incapable of explaining its emergence, which required a combinatorial explanation:

> *It was now clear that the eukaryotic cell was a genetic and biochemical mosaic, a hybrid cell in which basic, sub-cellular processes took place in physically separated compartments, each with a different evolutionary history, a history written in their genes. It was the start of a new era of molecular cell biological research, one freed from the constraints of "traditional" evolutionary thinking (Archibald 2016:86).*

Another major development in evolutionary biology has been the renewed emphasis on self-organisation, but as working with selection, not against it. The developmental biologist Stuart Kauffman argues that natural selection could only work if organisms were inherently "evolvable" in the first place. By this he means that they need to be self-organised so as to be able to evolve gradually and also possess redundancy or robustness, that is, able to tolerate numerous mutations that do not change the organism's behaviour:

> *If this view is roughly correct, then precisely that which is self-organised and robust is what we are likely to see pre-eminently utilised by selection. Then there is no necessary and fundamental conflict between self-organisation and selection. These two sources of order are natural partners. The cell membrane is a bilipid membrane,*

stable for almost 4 billion years both because it is robust and because such robust forms are readily malleable by natural selection.... The building blocks of life at a variety of levels from molecules to cells to tissues to organisms are precisely the robust, self-organised and emergent properties of the way the world works. If selection merely moulds further the stable properties of its building blocks, the emergent lawful order exhibited by such systems will persist in organisms (Kauffman 1995:188–9).

Again, the belief that the gene is the fundamental unit of selection is increasingly being rejected, and the idea of multilevel selection is taking its place, with a return of the idea not only of individual but also of group selection:

A theoretical framework emerged during the 1970s that could withstand the earlier criticisms. The framework has been empirically tested in both the laboratory and the field. A growing number of scientists now find it both uncontroversial and highly insightful to think of natural selection as a process that operates on a nested hierarchy of units. Multilevel selection theory is being used to explore an extraordinary range of phenomena, from the origin of life to the nature of human societies (Wilson 1997:52).

The existence of group "selection" has always been obvious in human society, from the clan to the tribe to the business corporation, but it is significant that it has now returned to mainstream evolutionary biology.

While these and other developments in evolutionary biology have often been bitterly resisted by orthodox neo-Darwinians, they are clearly more compatible with the theory of cultural evolution I have been advancing here. But these similarities do not require us to reduce culture to biology, that crude unification of the human and the physical sciences envisaged by the sociobiologists. On the contrary, once we think of evolution in terms of abstract structural transformations involving self-organisation, feedback, and equifinality we find a number of parallels and resemblances between the evolution of cultural and biological systems. Many of these were noted by Herbert Spencer and other nineteenth-century thinkers, and emphasise construction as just as important as selection.

Obvious examples are increasing centralisation of control, hierarchical structures, specialisation of function, and size both in biological and cultural evolution. We can also see obvious biological parallels to the cultural principles of evolutionary potential and the accumulation of necessary conditions. There is also group selection, lateral gene transfer which is combinatorial innovation, and the conservation of basic organic design whose analogous form in cultural evolution is core principles: "Organisms and societies both have means of conserving existing design features while adapting to change, so that the phylogenies of species and the history of particular cultures both display remarkable continuities despite a multitude of local variations. It is here, in the core principles of society, like the homeobox gene complexes, that a limited analogy of the genotype/phenotype distinction is really to be found" (Hallpike 2008b:291). Displaying continuity of design while undergoing change is also referred to as "robustness", and is found generally in culture, especially in technology, as well as in biology.

Whereas neo-Darwinism was obsessed with competition, and had great difficulty in accounting for co-operation, the new evolutionary biology with its adoption of symbiosis as a key process finds an obvious parallel with the strategic advantages of co-operation that make it universal in human culture. Again, there is an obvious parallel between the idea of "the survival of the mediocre" and Gould's "exaptation". I wrote: "Social evolution has therefore been possible partly because, instead of weeding out everything that is not immediately useful, societies carry a good deal of "dead wood" that may be of no particular adaptive value at the moment. They operate rather like those people who never throw anything away, because 'You never know when it may be useful'." (Hallpike 2008b:16). Unbeknown to me, Gould had already written in basically similar terms, although in rather more technical language: "...the enormous pool of non-aptations must be the well-spring and reservoir of most evolutionary flexibility. We need to recognise the central role of 'co-optability for fitness' as the primary evolutionary significance of ubiquitous non-aptation in organisms" (Gould & Vrba 1982:12).

All this suggests the value of a general, comparative study of evolutionary principles, regardless of whether they involve the inorganic, the organic, or the cultural levels of organisation. In conclusion, then, one may hope that this little book has managed to break the spell of the "Ionian Enchantment", and the illusion that all the complexities of biological and cultural evolution can be dissolved away by chanting some simple slogan like "Variation and Selection".

References

Abercrombie, M., *et al.* 1973. *The Penguin Dictionary of Biology.* 6th ed. London: Penguin.

Alexander, R. D. 1979. *Darwinism and Human Affairs.* University of Washington Press.

Anderson, S. R. & Lightfoot, D. W. 2000. "The human language faculty as an organ", *Annual Review of Physiology*, 62, 1–23.

Archibald, J. 2016. *One Plus One Equals One. Symbiosis and the evolution of complex life.* Oxford University Press.

Aunger, R. 2000. (ed.) *Darwinizing Culture: the status of memetics as a science.* Oxford University Press.

Barkow, J. H. 1978. "Culture and socio-biology". *American Anthropologist*, 80, 5–20.

Barnes, M. H. 2000. *Stages of Thought. The co-evolution of religious thought and science.* Oxford University Press.

Bellah, R. N. 1970. "Religious evolution" in *Beyond Belief. Essays on religion in a post-traditional world*, 20–45. New York: Harper & Row.

von Bertalannfy, L. 1971. *General System Theory.* London: Allen Lane The Penguin Press.

Blakemore, S. 1999. *The Meme Machine.* Oxford University Press.

Boehm, C. 1999. *Hierarchy in the Forest: the evolution of egalitarian behavior.* Harvard University Press.

Bray, F. (and J. Needham) 1984. *Science and Civilisation in China*, vol. 6 (2). Agriculture. Cambridge University Press.

Brown, D. E. 1991. *Human Universals.* New York: McGraw-Hill.

Caplow, T. 1957. "Organizational size", *Administrative Science Quarterly*, 1, 484–505.

Cavalli-Sforza, L. L. & Feldman, M. W. 1981. *Cultural Transmission and Evolution. A quantitative approach*. Princeton University Press.

Chagnon, N. A. 1967. "Yanomamo social organization and warfare", in *War*, eds. M. Fried *et al.* New York: Natural History Press.

Chomsky, N. 2010. "Some simple evo-devo theses: how true might they be for language?", in R. Larson, V. Déprez, & H. Yamakido (eds.), *The Evolution of Human Language*, 54–62. Cambridge University Press.

Claessen, H. J. M. 1978. "The early state: a structural approach", in *The Early State*, eds. H. J. M. Claesen and P. Skalnik, 535–96. The Hague: Mouton.

Cole, M., Gay, J., Glick, J., & Sharp, D. 1971. *The Cultural Context of Learning and Thinking*. London: Methuen.

Corning, P. A. 2005. *Holistic Darwinism. Synergy, Cybernetics, and the bioeconomics of evolution*. University of Chicago Press.

Damon, W. & Hart, D. 1988. *Self-Understanding in Childhood and Adolescence*. Cambridge University Press.

Darwin, C. 1902 [1872]. *The Origin of Species by means of natural selection*. 6th ed. London: Murray.

Darwin, C. 2011 [1871]. *The Descent of Man*. Pacific Publishing Studio.

Dawkins, R. 1978 [1976]. *The Selfish Gene*. London: Paladin Books.

Dawkins, R. 1986. *The Blind Watchmaker*. New York: Norton.

Dawkins, R. 1999. Foreword to Blakemore *The Meme Machine*, vii–xvii. Oxford University Press.

Dawkins, R. 2016. *The Extended Selfish Gene*. Oxford University Press.

Dennett, D. 1995. *Darwin's Dangerous Idea. Evolution and the meanings of life*. London: Penguin Books.

Denny, J. P. 1986. "Cultural ecology of mathematics: Ojibway and Inuit hunters", in (ed.) M. P. Closs, *Native American Mathematics*, 129–80.

Doidge, N. 2007. *The Brain that Changes Itself*. London: Penguin.

Durkheim, E. 1913. Review of L. Lévy-Bruhl's Les fonctions mentales dans les sociétés inférieures, *Année Sociologique*, 12, 33–7.

Durkheim, E. 1964. *The Rules of Sociological Method*. 8th ed. New York: Free Press.

Finley, M. I. 1973. *The Ancient Economy*. London: Chatto & Windus.

Flynn, J.R. 2007. *What is Intelligence? Beyond the Flynn effect*. Cambridge University.

Fondacaro, R., & Higgins, E. T. 1985. "Cognitive consequence of communication mode: a social psychological perspective", in *The Evolution of the Human Language. Biolinguistic perspectives*. (eds.) R. K. Larson et al., 73–90. Cambridge University Press.

Forbes, R. J. 1971. *Studies in Ancient Technology*. 2nd ed. Vol. VIII. Leiden: E. J. Brill.

Forth, G. 1982. "The expression of temporality in eastern Sumba", *Ethnos*, 47, 232–48.

Fracchia, J., & Lewontin, R. C. 1999. "Does culture evolve?", *History and Theory*, 38, 52–78.

Fracchia, J., & Lewontin, R. C. 2005. "Does culture evolve?: The price of metaphor", *History and Theory*, 44, 14–29.

von Fürer-Haimendorf, C. 1967. *Morals and Merit. A study of values and social controls in South Asian societies*. London: Weidenfeld & Nicolson.

Flynn, J. R. 2007. *What is Intelligence? Beyond the Flynn effect*. Cambridge University Press.

Gaulin, S. J. C. & Schlegel, A. (1980). "Paternal confidence and paternal investment: a cross-cultural test of a sociobiological hypothesis." *Ethnology and Sociobiology*, 1(4), 301–9.

Gay, J., & and Cole, M. 1967. *The New Mathematics and an Old Culture*. New York: Holt, Rinehart, Winston.

Gibbs, J. C. et al. 2007. "Moral judgment across cultures. Revisiting Kohlberg's universality claims", *Developmental Review*, 27, 443–500.

Ginsberg, M. 1944. *Moral Progress*. Frazer Lecture. Glasgow University Press.

Gluckman, M. 1949. "Social beliefs and individual thinking in primitive society", *Memoirs and Proceedings of the Manchester Literary and Philosophical Society*, 91, 73–98.

Goldman, I. 1970. *Ancient Polynesian Society*. University of Chicago Press.

Gontier, N. (2016) "Symbiogenesis, History of" in Kliman, R. M. (ed.), *Encyclopedia of Evolutionary Biology.* vol. 4, pp. 261–271. Oxford: Academic Press.

Gorst, J. E. 2001. *The Maori King*. Auckland: Reed Books.

Gould, S. J., and Vrba, E. 1982. "Exaptation—a missing term in the science of form", *Palaeobiology*, 8(1), 4–15.

Hage, P., & Harary, F. 1983. *Structural Models in Anthropology*. Cambridge University Press.

Hallpike, C. R. 1970. "The principles of alliance formation between Konso towns", *Man*, 5(2), 258–80.

Hallpike, C. R. 1973. "Functionalist interpretations of primitive warfare", *Man*, 8(3), 451–70.

Hallpike, C. R. 1977. *Bloodshed and Vengeance in the Papuan Mountains. The generation of conflict in Tauade society.* Oxford: Clarendon Press.

Hallpike, C. R. 1979 *The Foundations of Primitive Thought*. Oxford: Clarendon Press.

Hallpike, C. R. 1984. "The relevance of the theory of inclusive fitness to human society". *Journal of Social and Biological Structures*, 7, 131–144.

Hallpike, C. R. 1986. *The Principles of Social Evolution*. Oxford: Clarendon Press.

Hallpike, C. R. 2008a. [1972] *The Konso of Ethiopia. A study of the values of an East Cushitic society.* Revised edition. Bloomington, Indiana and Milton Keynes: AuthorHouse.

Hallpike, C. R. 2008b. *How We Got Here. From bows and arrows to the space age.* Bloomington, Indiana and Milton Keynes: AuthorHouse.

Hallpike, C. R. 2011. *On Primitive Society, and other forbidden topics.* Bloomington, Indiana and Milton Keynes: AuthorHouse.

Hallpike, C. R. 2016. *Ethical Thought in Increasingly Complex Societies. Social structure and moral development.* Lanham, New York, London: Lexington Books.

Hallpike, C. R. 2018a. *Ship of Fools. An anthology of learned nonsense about primitive society.* Kouvola, Finland: Castalia House.

Hallpike, C. R. 2018b. "So all languages aren't equally complex after all", in *Ship of Fools*, 121–173.

Harris, M. 1978. *Cannibals and Kings. The origins of cultures.* London: Collins.

Harris, M. 1980. *Cultural Materialism. The struggle for a science of culture.* New York: Vintage Books.

Hauser, M. D. 2006. *Moral Minds: How nature designed our universal sense of right and wrong.* New York: Harper Collins.

Hobhouse, L. T. 1929. *Morals in Evolution.* 6th ed. London: Chapman & Hall.

Holmes, G. 1992. Foreword to *The Oxford History of Medieval Europe.* Oxford University Press.

Huxley, J. 1956. "Evolution, cultural and biological", in *Current Anthropology*, ed. W. L. Thomas, 3–25. University of Chicago Press.

Huxley, J. 1974. *Evolution. The modern synthesis.* 3rd ed. London: Allen & Unwin.

Ibbotson, P., & Tomasello, M. 2016. "Language in a new key", *Scientific American*, November, 71–75.

Ingold, T. 2000. "The poverty of selectionism", *Anthropology Today*, 16(3), 1–2.

Kauffman, S. 1995. *At Home in the Universe. The search for the laws of self-organization and complexity.* Oxford University Press.

Kelley, D. B. 2013. *The Origin of Everything via Universal Selection, or the Preservation of Favored Systems in Contention for Existence.* Newbury, Ohio: Woodhollow Press.

King, A., & Crewe, I. 2013. *The Blunders of Our Governments.* London: Oneworld Publications.

Kirch, P. V. & Green, R. C. 2001. *Hawaiki, Ancestral Polynesia. An essay in historical anthropology.* Cambridge University Press.

Kluckhohn, C. 1960. "The moral order in the expanding society", in *City Invincible. A symposium in urbanization and cultural development in the ancient Near East.* eds. C. H. Kraeling & R. M. Adams, 391–404. University of Chicago Press.

Kohlberg, L. 1984. *The Psychology of Moral Development. The nature and validity of moral stages.* San Francisco: Harper & Row.

Kuhn, T. S. 1957. *The Copernican Revolution.* Harvard University Press.

Laland, K. N., & Brown, G. R. 2002. *Sense and Nonsense. Evolutionary perspectives on human behaviour.* Oxford University Press.

Lewis, H. S. 1974. "Neighbours, friends, and kinsmen: principles of social organization among the Cushitic-speaking peoples of Ethiopia". *Ethnology*, 13, 145–57.

Lewontin, R. C. 1957. "The adaptation of population to varying environments", *Cold Springs Harbor Symposia in Quantitative Biology*, 22, 395–408.

Lewontin, R. C. 1979. "Sociobiology as an adaptationist program", *Behavioral Science*, 24, 5–14.

Lewontin, R. C. 1984. "Adaptation", in *Conceptual Issues in Evolutionary Biology*, ed. E. Sober, 234–51. MIT Press.

Lienhardt, G. 1961. *Divinity and Experience. The religion of the Dinka.* Oxford: Clarendon Press.

Littlejohn, J. 1963. "Temne space", *Anthropological Quarterly*, 36, 1–17.

Lumsden, C. J., & Wilson, E. O. 1981. *Genes, Mind, and Culture. The coevolutionary process*. Harvard University Press.

Luria, A. R. 1976. *Cognitive Development. Its cultural and social foundations*. Harvard University Press.

Malinowski, B. 1922. *Argonauts of the Western Pacific*. London: Routledge & Kegan Paul.

Malinowski, B. 1926. "Anthropology", *Encyclopedia Britannica* 13th ed. Supp. Vol. I, 131–40.

McGilchrist, I. 2012. *The Master and His Emissary. The divided brain and the making of the western world*. Yale University Press.

Matthew, P. 1831. *Naval Timber and Arboriculture*. Edinburgh: Adam & Charles Black.

Mesoudi, A., Whiten, A., & Laland, K. N. 2004. "Perspective: is human cultural evolution Darwinian? Evidence reviewed from the perspective of The Origin of Species." *Evolution*, 58. 1–11.

Mesoudi, A. 2008. "Foresight in cultural evolution". *Biology and Philosophy*, 23(2), 243–55.

Mesoudi, A. 2016. "Cultural evolution: a review of theory, findings and controversies", *Evolutionary Biology*, 43, 481–97.

Moore, O. K. 1957. "Divination—a new perspective", *American Anthropologist*, 59, 69–74.

Murphy, R. F. 1957. "Intergroup hostility and social cohesion", *American Anthropologist*, 59, 1018–35.

Needham, R. 1962. *Structure and Sentiment. A test case in social anthropology*. University of Chicago Press.

Noble, D. 2018. "Central dogma or central debate?", *Physiology*, 33, 246–249.

North, J. 2005. *God's Clockmaker. Richard of Wallingford and the invention of time*. London: Hambledon & London.

Onians, R. B. 1954. *The Origins of Modern European Thought*. Cambridge University Press.

Overing, J. 1985. "Introduction" to *Reason and Morality*. ed. J. Overing. 1–28, ASA Monographs 24. London: Tavistock.

Piaget, J. 1930. *The Child's Conception of Physical Causality*. London: Routledge & Kegan Paul.

Piaget, J. 1952. *The Child's Conception of Number*. London: Routledge & Kegan Paul.

Piaget, J. 1970 [1932]. *The Moral Judgment of the Child*. London: Routledge & Kegan Paul.

Piaget, J. 1971. *Structuralism*. tr. and ed. C. Maschler, London: Routledge & Kegan Paul.

Piaget, J. 1977 [1955]. "The stages of intellectual development in childhood and adolescence" in *The Essential Piaget*, eds. H. Gruber & J. Voneche, 814–19. London: Routledge & Kegan Paul.

Pinker, S. 1997. *How the Mind Works*. London: Penguin.

Pinker, S. 2015. *The Language Instinct. How the mind creates language*. London: Penguin.

Popper, K. 1957. *The Poverty of Historicism*. London: Routledge & Kegan Paul.

Prince, J. R. 1969. *Science Concepts in a Pacific Culture*. Sydney: Angus & Robertson.

Rappaport, R. A. 1968. *Pigs for the Ancestors. Ritual in the ecology of a New Guinea people*. Yale University Press.

Read, K. E. 1955. "Morality and the conception of the person among the Gahuku-Gama", *Oceania* 25(4), 233–82.

Rees, M. 1998. "The evolution of the universe", in *Evolution. Society, science, and the universe*. ed. A. Fabian, 136–150. Cambridge University Press.

Resnik, D. 1994. "The rebirth of rational morphology", *Acta Biotheoretica*, 42(1), 1–14.

Richerson, P. J. & Boyd, R. 1985. *Culture and the Evolutionary Process*. University of Chicago Press.

Richerson, P. J. & Boyd, R. 2006. *Not by Genes Alone. How culture transformed human evolution*. University of Chicago Press.

Russell, B. 1948. *Human Knowledge: Its Scope and Limits*. London: Allen & Unwin.

Russell, B. 1955. *History of Western Philosophy*. London: Allen & Unwin.

Sahlins, M. 1961. "The segmentary lineage: an organization of predatory expansion", *American Anthropologist*, 63, 322–45.

Sahlins, M. 1963. "Poor man, rich man, big-man, chief: political types in Melanesia and Polynesia", *Comparative Studies in Society and History*, 5(3), 285–303.

Sahlins, M. 1977. *The Use and Abuse of Biology. An anthropological critique of sociobiology.* London: Tavistock.

Sampson, G. 2009. "A linguistic axiom challenged", in *Language Complexity as an Evolving Variable*, 1–18. Oxford University Press.

Sanderson, S. K. 2001. *The Evolution of Human Society. A Darwinian conflict perspective.* Lanham: Rowman & Littlefield.

Schneider, D. M. 1961. "The distinctive features of matrilineal descent groups", in *Matrilineal Kinship*, eds. D. M. Schneider & M. Gough, 1–29. University of California Press.

Simpson, G. G. 1953. *The Major Features of Evolution.* Columbia University Press.

Skinner, B. F. 1971. *Beyond Freedom and Dignity.* Indianapolis: Hackett.

Skinner, B. F. 1974. *About Behaviorism.* London: Jonathan Cape.

Snarey, J. R. 1985. "Cross-cultural universality of social-moral development: a critical review of Kohlbergian research", *Psychological Bulletin*, 97, 202–32.

Sperber, D. 2000. "An objection to the memetic approach to culture", in *Darwinizing Culture*, ed. R. Aunger, 163–73. Oxford University Press.

Stewart, I. 2011. *The Mathematics of Life.* New York: Basic Books.

Straube, H. 1963. *West Kuschitsche Völker Süd-Äthiopiens.* Stuttgart: Kohlhammer.

Tiger, L., & Fox, R. 1971. *The Imperial Animal.* Toronto: McClelland & Stewart.

Tomasello, M. 2009. *Why We Cooperate.* MIT Press.

Tooby, J., and Cosmides, L. 1992. "The psychological foundations of culture", in (eds.) J. Barkow, L. Cosmides, and J. Tooby, *The Adapted Mind. Evolutionary psychology and the generation of culture*, 19–136. Oxford University Press.

Trigger, B. 1972. "Determinants of urban growth in pre-industrial societies", in *Man, Settlement and Urbanism*, eds. P. J. Ucko et al. 576–99. London: Duckworth.

Trigger, B. 1990. *Understanding Ancient Civilizations*. Cambridge University Press.

Trivers, R. L. 1971. "The evolution of reciprocal altruism". *Quarterly Review of. Biology*, 46, 35–57.

Turney-High, H. H. 1971. *Primitive War. Its practice and concepts*. University of South Carolina Press.

Uttal, W. R. 2001. *The New Phrenology. The limits of localizing cognitive processes in the brain*. MIT Press.

Vayda, A. P. 1971. "Phases of the process of war and peace among the Marings of New Guinea", *Oceania* 42, 1–24.

Wade, N. 2007. *Before the Dawn. Recovering the lost history of our ancestors*. London: Duckworth.

Wagner, A. 2014. *Arrival of the Fittest. Solving evolution's greatest puzzle*. New York: Current.

Wallace, A. R. 1871. "The limits of Natural Selection as applied to Man", Chapter X in his *Contributions to the Theory of Natural Selection*, 2nd edn. 332–71. London: Macmillan.

Williams, G. C. 1966. *Adaptation and Natural Selection. A critique of some current evolutionary thought*. Princeton University Press.

Wilson, D. S. 1997. "Multilevel selection theory comes of age", *The American Naturalist*, 150 (51), 51–54.

Wilson, E. O. 1998. *Consilience. The unity of knowledge*. New York: Little Brown.

Wilson, E. O. 2004. *On Human Nature*. 2nd ed. Harvard University Press.

Wrangham, R. 2009. *Catching Fire. How cooking made us human*. London: Profile Books.

About the Author

C. R. Hallpike is an English and Canadian anthropologist whose work covers a period of fifty years, and is unusually wide-ranging and diverse. Apart from extensive field work in Ethiopia and Papua New Guinea, he has made distinctive contributions to some of the most fundamental problems in the subject: cultural relativism, social evolution, primitive thought, the nature of religion, warfare, moral development, and even the origins of modern science.

NON-FICTION

4D Warfare by Jack Posobiec
The Last Closet by Moira Greyland
The Nine Laws by Ivan Throne
SJWs Always Lie by Vox Day
SJWs Always Double Down by Vox Day
Collected Columns, Vol. I: Innocence & Intellect, 2001—2005 by Vox Day
Collected Columns, Vol. II: Crisis & Conceit, 2005—2009 by Vox Day
The LawDog Files by LawDog
The LawDog Files: African Adventures by LawDog
Equality: The Impossible Quest by Martin van Creveld
A History of Strategy by Martin van Creveld
Between Light and Shadow by Marc Aramini

MILITARY SCIENCE FICTION

There Will Be War Volumes I and II ed. Jerry Pournelle
Starship Liberator by David VanDyke and B. V. Larson
Battleship Indomitable by David VanDyke and B. V. Larson
The Eden Plague by David VanDyke
Reaper's Run by David VanDyke
Skull's Shadows by David VanDyke

FICTION

Turned Earth: A Jack Broccoli Novel by David T. Good
An Equation of Almost Infinite Complexity by J. Mulrooney
The Missionaries by Owen Stanley
The Promethean by Owen Stanley
Brings the Lightning by Peter Grant
Rocky Mountain Retribution by Peter Grant
Hitler in Hell by Martin van Creveld

SCIENCE FICTION

Soda Pop Soldier by Nick Cole
CTRL-ALT Revolt! by Nick Cole
Superluminary by John C. Wright
City Beyond Time by John C. Wright
Back From the Dead by Rolf Nelson
Mutiny in Space by Rod Walker
Alien Game by Rod Walker
Young Man's War by Rod Walker